LIBRARY OF CONGRESS

Manuscripts

AN ILLUSTRATED GUIDE

LIBRARY OF CONGRESS WASHINGTON 1993

This publication was made possible by generous support from the James Madison Council, a national, private-sector advisory council dedicated to helping the Library of Congress share its unique resources with the nation and the world.

The guide is composed in Centaur, a typeface designed by American typographer and book designer Bruce Rogers (1870−1957). The full type font was first used at the Montague Press in 1915 for an edition of Maurice de Guérin's *The Centaur.*

The guide was designed by Robert Wiser and Laurie Rosenthal, Meadows & Wiser, Washington, D.C.

COVER: A detail from the first page of the "original Rough draft" of the Declaration of Independence in Thomas Jefferson's own hand. *(Thomas Jefferson Papers)*

·LIBRARY OF CONGRESS CATALOGING-IN-PUBLICATION DATA

Library of Congress.
    Library of Congress manuscripts : an illustrated guide.
       p. cm.
    ISBN 0-8444-0798-4
      1. Manuscripts — Washington (D. C.) — Catalogs. 2. Library of Congress — Catalogs. I. Title.
    Z6621.U58L53   1993
    [Z663.34]
    016.091'0973 — dc20   93−2529
                                                CIP

For sale by the U.S. Government Printing Office
Superintendent of Documents, Mail Stop: SSOP, Washington, DC 20402-9328
ISBN 0-16-041873-9

Contents

A Declaration by the Representatives of the UNITED STATES
OF AMERICA, in General Congress assembled.

When in the course of human events it becomes necessary for one people to
dissolve the political bands which have connected them with another, and to as-
-sume among the powers of the earth the separate and equal station to
which the laws of nature & of nature's god entitle them, a decent respect
to the opinions of mankind requires that they should declare the causes
which impel them to the separation.

We hold these truths to be self-evident; that all men are
created equal, that they are endowed by their creator with
inherent & inalienable rights; that among these are
life, liberty, & the pursuit of happiness; that to secure these rights, go
-vernments are instituted among men, deriving their just powers from
the consent of the governed; that whenever any form of government
becomes destructive of these ends, it is the right of the people to alter
or to abolish it, & to institute new government, laying it's foundation on
such principles & organising it's powers in such form, as to them shall
seem most likely to effect their safety & happiness. prudence indeed
will dictate that governments long established should not be changed for
light & transient causes: and accordingly all experience hath shewn that
mankind are more disposed to suffer while evils are sufferable, than to
right themselves by abolishing the forms to which they are accustomed. but
when a long train of abuses & usurpations [begun at a distinguished period,
&] pursuing invariably the same object, evinces a design to reduce
them + under absolute Despotism, it is their right, it is their duty, to throw off such
+ & to provide new guards for their future security. such has
been the patient sufferance of these colonies; & such is now the necessity
which constrains them to expunge their former systems of government.
the history of the present King of Great Britain is a history of unremitting injuries and
usurpations, among which appears no solitary fact to contra-
-dict the uniform tenor of the rest, all of which have in direct object the
establishment of an absolute tyranny over these states. to prove this, let facts be
submitted to a candid world, for the truth of which we pledge a faith
yet unsullied by falsehood.

as. refused his assent to laws the most wholesome and necessary for the pub-
-lic good:

has forbidden his governors to pass laws of immediate & pressing importance,

unless suspended in their operation till his assent should be obtained;

and when so suspended, he has utterly neglected utterly to attend to them.

as refused to pass other laws for the accommodation of large districts of people

unless those people would relinquish the right of representation in the legislature, a right

inestimable to them & formidable to tyrants only:

he has called together legislative bodies at places unusual, unco-

he has dissolving of their public records for the sole purpose of fati-

with measures:

he has refused for a long time after such dissolutions to cause others to be elected,

whereby the legislative powers, incapable of annihilation, have returned to

the people at large for their exercise, the state remaining in the mean time

exposed to all the dangers of invasion from without & convulsions within:

has endeavored to prevent the population of these states; for that purpose

obstructing the laws for naturalization of foreigners; refusing to pass others

to encourage their migrations hither, & raising the conditions of new ap-

-propriations of lands:

has suffered the administration of justice totally to cease in some of these

estates refusing his assent to laws for establishing judiciary powers:

has made our judges dependant on his will alone, for the tenure of their offices,

and the amount of their salaries: the + & payment

has erected a multitude of new offices [by a self-assumed power] & sent hi-

-ther swarms of officers to harrass our people & eat out their substance:

has kept among us in times of peace standing armies [& ships of war] without the consent of our legislatures

has affected to render the military independent of & superior to the civil power:

has combined with others to subject us to a jurisdiction foreign to our constitu-

-tions and unacknoleged by our laws; giving his assent to their acts of pretended

& legislation, for quartering large bodies of armed troops among us;

for protecting them by a mock-trial from punishment for any murders

which they should commit on the inhabitants of these states;

for cutting off our trade with all parts of the world;

for imposing taxes on us without our consent;

for depriving us in many cases of the benefits of trial by jury;

for transporting us beyond seas to be tried for pretended offences:

for abolishing the free system of English laws in a neighboring province, establishing therein an arbitrary government,

and enlarging it's boundaries so as to render it at once an example & fit instrument for introducing the same absolute

* mr Adams

+ Dr Franklin

abolishing our most ~~important~~ Laws

for taking away our charters & altering fundamentally the forms of our government

for suspending our own legislatures & declaring themselves invested with power to

legislate for us in all cases whatsoever.

he has abdicated government here, [by declaring us out of his protection & waging war against us. withdrawing his governors, & declaring us out

of his allegiance & protection:]

he has plundered our seas, ravaged our coasts, burnt our towns & destroyed the

lives of our people:

he is at this time transporting large armies of foreign mercenaries to complete

~~the works of death, desolation & tyranny, already begun with circumstances~~ Scotch and other

~~scarcely paralleled in the most barbarous ages, & totally~~

of cruelty & perfidy, unworthy the head of a civilized nation:

he has endeavored to bring on the inhabitants of our frontiers the merciless Indian

savages, whose known rule of warfare is an undistinguished destruction of

all ages, sexes, & conditions [of existence:]

[he has incited treasonable insurrections of our fellow-~~citizens~~, with the

allurements of forfeiture & confiscation of our property.

he has waged cruel war against human nature itself, violating it's most sa-

-cred rights of life & liberty in the persons of a distant people who never of-

fended him, captivating & carrying them into slavery in another hemi-

-sphere, or to incur miserable death in their transportation thither. this

piratical warfare, the opprobrium of infidel powers, is the warfare of the

Christian king of Great Britain. determined to keep open a market

where MEN should be bought & sold, he has prostituted his negative

for suppressing every legislative attempt to prohibit or to restrain this

~~determining to keep open a market where MEN should be bought & sold:~~

execrable commerce: and that this assemblage of horrors might want no fact

of distinguished die, he is now exciting those very people to rise in arms

among us, and to purchase that liberty of which he has deprived them

by ~~depriving them~~ murdering the people upon whom he also obtruded them: thus paying

off former crimes committed against the liberties of one people, with crimes

which he urges them to commit against the lives of another.]

in every stage of these oppressions we have petitioned for redress in the most humble

terms; our repeated petitions have been answered only by repeated injuries. a prince

whose character is thus marked by every act which may define a tyrant, is unfit

to be the ruler of a people ~~who mean to be~~ free. future ages will scarce believe

that the hardiness of one man, adventured within the short compass of twelve years

only, ~~to lay a foundation so broad & undisguised for tyranny~~ over a people fostered & fixed in principles

of ~~liberty~~ freedom.]

Nor have we been wanting in attentions to our British brethren. we have
warned them from time to time of attempts by their legislature to extend a juris-
-diction over [these our states]. we have reminded them of the circumstances of
our emigration & settlement here, [no one of which could warrant so strange a
pretension: that these were effected at the expence of our own blood & treasure,
unassisted by the wealth or the strength of Great Britain: that in constituting
indeed our several forms of government, we had adopted one common king, thereby
laying a foundation for perpetual league & amity with them: but that submission to their

credited: and we appealed to their native justice & magnanimity, as well as to the ties
of our common kindred to disavow these usurpations which were likely to interrupt
our correspondence & connection. they too have been deaf to the voice of justice &
of consanguinity. & when occasions have been given them, by the regular course of
their laws, of removing from their councils the disturbers of our harmony, they
have by their free election re-established them in power. at this very time too they
are permitting their chief magistrate to send over not only soldiers of our common
blood, but Scotch & foreign mercenaries to invade & destroy us. these facts
have given the last stab to agonizing affection, and manly spirit bids us to re-
-nounce for ever these unfeeling brethren. we must endeavor to forget our former
love for them, and to hold them as we hold the rest of mankind, enemies in war,
in peace friends. we might have been a free & a great people together; but a commu-
-nication of grandeur & of freedom it seems is below their dignity. be it so, since they
will have it: the road to happiness & to glory is open to us too; we will tread it
apart from them, and acquiesce in the necessity which denounces our
eternal separation!

We therefore the representatives of the United States of America in General Con-
-gress assembled, do in the name & by authority of the good people of these states,
reject & renounce all allegiance & subjection to the kings of Great Britain
& all others who may hereafter claim by, through, or under them; we utterly
dissolve all political connection which may heretofore have sub-
-sisted between us & the people or parliament of Great Britain; and finally
we do assert and declare these colonies to be free and independant states,
and that as free & independant states they have full power to levy
war, conclude peace, contract alliances, establish commerce, & to do all other
acts and things which independant states may of right do. And for the
support of this declaration we mutually pledge to each other our lives, our
fortunes, & our sacred honour.

Introduction

PRECEDING PAGES. One of the Library's rarest treasures is the "original Rough draft" of the Declaration of Independence in Thomas Jefferson's own hand. On 11 June 1776, Jefferson, John Adams, Benjamin Franklin, Roger Sherman, and Robert L. Livingston were appointed to a committee of the Continental Congress "to prepare the declaration." The four-page manuscript in Jefferson's handwriting may have been a clean copy of earlier creative drafts prepared by him, which no longer exist. Jefferson's draft was submitted to the committee members, and it bears the emendations made first by Adams and Franklin and later by the whole Congress before its final adoption on 4 July 1776. (*Thomas Jefferson Papers*)

MANY OF THE COUNTRY's earliest leaders recognized the historical significance of their papers, none more so than Thomas Jefferson, who in 1823 wrote that it was "the duty of every good citizen to use all the opportunities, which occur to him, for preserving documents relating to the history of our country."[1] Jefferson meticulously cared for his own papers and actively collected documents relating to the early history of Virginia and the United States. In fact, when Congress purchased Jefferson's library in 1815 to replace the earlier library burned by British troops during the War of 1812, important manuscript records were included among the books and maps. These earliest manuscripts acquired by the Library of Congress concerned the Virginia Company of London, the commercial body that founded—and for a short time governed—the oldest English-speaking colony in North America, Jefferson's beloved commonwealth of Virginia.

After Jefferson's death, the Library purchased at auction in 1829 the president's remaining collection of Virginia Company records. In the 164 years since the second Jefferson acquisition, the Library has amassed an unparalleled collection of manuscripts. Some of these are housed in the Library's music, rare book, and area studies divisions, but most are in the custody of the Manuscript Division, one of the original departments established in 1897, when the Library moved across the street from its cramped quarters in the United States Capitol to its own magnificent new structure, later appropriately named the Thomas Jefferson Building.

The first chief of the Manuscript Division estimated that the size of his collections was twenty-five thousand items. Today, nearly a century later, the division holds ten thousand collections containing more than fifty million items. These collections document all aspects of American history and culture and include some of the nation's greatest manuscript treasures. Among these are Jefferson's rough draft of the Declaration of Independence, James Madison's notes on the Constitutional Convention, the paper tape of the first telegraphic message, Abraham Lincoln's Gettysburg Address, Alexander Graham Bell's first drawing of the telephone, and similar items recording dramatic events in the nation's history. Represented are the papers of most of the presidents of the United States, their Cabinet ministers, many of their colleagues and adversaries in the Senate and House of Representatives, members of the Supreme Court and federal judiciary, military officers and diplomats, artists and writers, scientists and inventors, and other prominent Americans whose lives reflect our country's evolution.

The overwhelming majority of the division's collections comprise the personal papers of individuals and families. They differ from the holdings of the National Archives and Records Administration, which maintains the official records of the United States government. The most interesting of the Manuscript Division's collections relate not only to individuals' professional or political careers but reflect their private lives, suggesting how their origins, family relationships, personal experiences, motivations, prejudices, and humor affected their public behavior and activities. As a record of the whole person, these collections contain many different types of manuscripts. Included are diaries, correspondence (both incoming and copies of outgoing letters), notebooks, accounts, logs, scrapbooks, press clippings, subject files, photographs, and other documents in every conceivable form—handwritten and typewritten, originals, carbons, letterpress copies, microfilm, and computer diskettes. When the poet Carl Sandburg wrote about the private Lincoln collection of Oliver Barrett, he could just as easily have been describing the papers in the Manuscript Division:

Many kinds of paper here—heavy parchment and vellum engrossed—legal cap—letter and note paper—scrap—newsprint of the later era now beginning to disintegrate—rag paper of the previous generation, tough and fibrous and good for centuries to come with its register of handwriting or printing—quiet paper that whispers its tender message, or groaning, roaring paper that for those of imagination carries its own grief or elation of a vanished hour and day. Paper, if you please, sir or madam, as soundless as hushed footfalls on silent snow.[2]

Although interesting as artifacts, the real worth of the manuscripts in the Library of Congress lies in their evidentiary value. They are the primary sources upon which the writing of history is based. They permit scholars to reconstruct and understand the past, interpret the national character, and set the record straight about events and personalities often shrouded in mystery and steeped in controversy. The historical value of the Library's manuscripts is enhanced by their scope, size, and concentration in one place. A scholar planning initially to consult one collection will be drawn to a complementary collection containing documents which clarify, enhance, and contradict the first set of manuscripts. It is rare for patrons to leave the Manuscript Division without finding something relevant to their research. Moreover, the Library's manuscripts are housed in immediate proximity to the institution's unsurpassed collections of books, pamphlets, magazines, newspapers, maps, motion pictures, charts, prints, sound recordings, and photographs that can supplement the scholar's manuscript research.

Manuscripts are normally acquired by the Library of Congress in one of

Although most of the Manuscript Division's collections comprise the papers of nationally prominent individuals, ordinary men and women are also represented, especially among our military collections, many of which include correspondence between family members separated by war. Shown here is a Civil War letter from Charles Wellington Reed (1841–1926) to his mother. Reed, a private in the Ninth Massachusetts Light Artillery, frequently decorated his letters home with pencil sketches of army life. His artistic talent gained him a position in the Topographic Engineers, Army of the Potomac. (*Charles W. Reed Papers*)

my ribs will all get old Markeny - that is, they will look like sale molasses in time - my water colors will fade - but - I am to endure in bronze - even rust does not touch. - I am modeling - I find I do well - I am doing a cow boy on a bucking bronco and I am going to rattle down through all the ages, unless some American boids the old marsan and knock I off the shelf.

In this second page of an undated letter to western writer Owen Wister, Frederic Remington — sculptor, illustrator, and painter — muses about the permanence of his bronze sculptures and the instability of his oil paintings and watercolors. The ink sketch of Remington's famous bronze Bronco Buster, on which he had just begun work (ca. 1894), documents the artist's ambition to record the vanishing West during his extensive travels. (*Owen Wister Papers*)

three ways: purchase, gift, or copyright deposit. Many of the earliest acquisitions were purchased by the Library directly or transferred from other government agencies. For example, in 1867 Congress appropriated $100,000 to purchase the Peter Force Papers, one of the nation's first great privately assembled manuscript collections. A year earlier, Dolley Madison's papers had been transferred from the Smithsonian Institution, and in 1903 President Theodore Roosevelt signed an executive order directing the transfer to the Manuscript Division of the State Department's historical archives. Roosevelt's action, one of the most significant in the division's history, brought to the Library the major corpus of the papers of George Washington, Thomas Jefferson, James Madison, and James Monroe, as well as large bodies of the papers of Benjamin Franklin and Alexander Hamilton. Funds established by private benefactors also permitted the Library to purchase manuscripts unobtainable within the budget appropriated by Congress, including the papers of poet Walt Whitman, artist James A. McNeill Whistler, and psychoanalyst Sigmund Freud, as well as copies of records in foreign repositories relating to American history.

Notwithstanding these notable purchases, most of the Manuscript Division's acquisitions in the twentieth century have been donated or, in the case of microfilm, acquired through copyright deposit. Many prominent Americans have accepted the division's invitation to donate their papers to the national library during their lifetimes. Other collections have been bequeathed or received as gifts from heirs. Only through the generosity of countless donors has the Manuscript Division amassed one of the world's finest collections of historical manuscripts. As such, our holdings are a testament to the patriotism of the American people.

Once acquired, an expert processing staff sorts, arranges, and describes incoming collections — occasionally discovering in the process locks of hair, articles of clothing, revolvers, jewelry, pressed flowers, pieces of wedding cakes, badges, pins, and other oddities accidently donated with the manuscripts. The organized collections are stored in acid-free folders within similarly treated containers to retard deterioration. The containers are then shelved in secure, fireproof stacks with temperature and humidity controls. Damaged items are repaired and restored by talented and knowledgeable specialists in the Library's state-of-the-art conservation facilities.

The ease with which a collection is organized depends upon the condition and order of the manuscripts upon receipt. Many present-day archivists can appreciate former President Madison's despair that the "tedious" arrangement of his papers was absorbing more of his time than anticipated, interfering, he added, with the enjoyment of his retirement.[3] During the third winter that her husband devoted to his manuscripts, Dolley Madison restlessly noted that "the business seems to accumulate as he proceeds, so that it might outlast my patience, and yet I cannot press him to forsake a duty so important, or find it in my heart to leave him during its fulfillment."[4] Careful arrangement and accurate description are indeed time-consuming and important tasks. Both contribute to a collection's preservation, security, and accessibility for research use.

Once collections are processed, they are made available within established guidelines to interested scholars in the Manuscript Division Reading Room. Professional librarians and subject specialists are available to advise patrons about new avenues of research, direct them to relevant source materials, and answer reference queries about the division's holdings.

Mining the treasures of the Manuscript Division is a lifelong pursuit for researchers and staff alike. Longtime employees are constantly amazed by both the documented riches and the unexpected finds. The thrill of discovering the unknown, the excitement of handling famous documents, and the feeling of connectedness with people and events of the past are among the most satisfying aspects of archival work. Through the Library's diverse collection of manuscripts, history comes alive, attaining an immediacy that is both unique and rewarding for anyone who ventures into the Manuscript Division's holdings. Letters and diaries—from both the recent and the distant past—speak of a nation's hopes, disappointments, and accomplishments. The style and modes of expression differ markedly, but whether eloquent or crude, these manuscripts transport the reader to a time and place that may be radically different from the present or, conversely, seem either frighteningly or comfortingly familiar. By collecting, preserving, and making available for research use documents of the American past, the Manuscript Division promotes the pursuit of knowledge that is central to all great civilizations. We are proud to serve as custodians of the nation's historical legacy and invite you to learn more about the division's holdings in the following pages.

JAMES H. HUTSON, CHIEF
MANUSCRIPT DIVISION

The following staff members contributed to this guide: Alice L. Birney, Gerard W. Gawalt, Debra Newman Ham, John E. Haynes, Marvin W. Kranz, John J. McDonough, Janice E. Ruth, John R. Sellers, and David Wigdor.

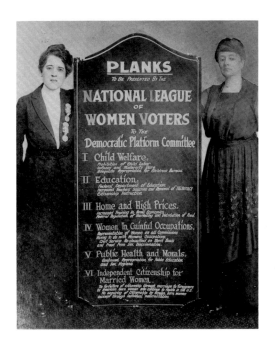

Maud Wood Park *(right)*, first president of the National League of Women Voters (LWV), displays the planks the organization urged on the Democratic Platform Committee in the 1920 presidential election, the first in which women could vote. The LWV evolved from the National American Woman Suffrage Association, and the Library holds the papers of both groups and of many of their leaders. *(Maud Wood Park Papers)*

This painting is one of eight Indian paintings from the 1531 Huejotzingo Codex, part of the documentation in a legal action brought by the conqueror of Mexico, Hernán Cortés, against members of the first audiencia or the Spanish high court in Mexico, who earlier had tried to take over Cortés's land and power. The eight paintings in the codex illustrate the testimony of Indians called as witnesses in the case. This painting illustrates the contributions of the Huejotzingo people to Cortés's conquest of New Galicia. The image of the Madonna and Child framed in the blue rectangle represents the standard of the expedition's leader, Nuño de Guzman, and is one of the earliest native references to Christianity. *(Edward S. Harkness Collection)*

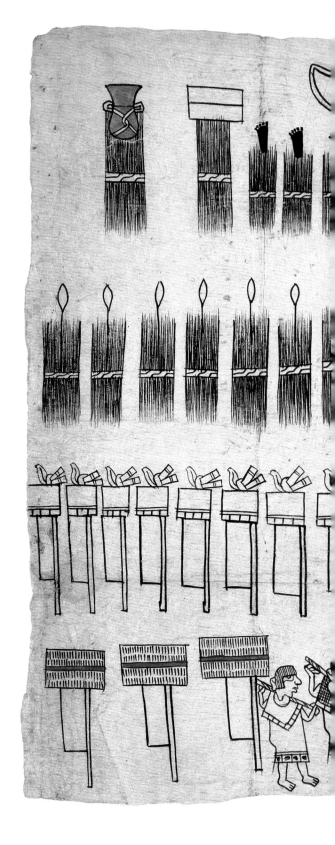

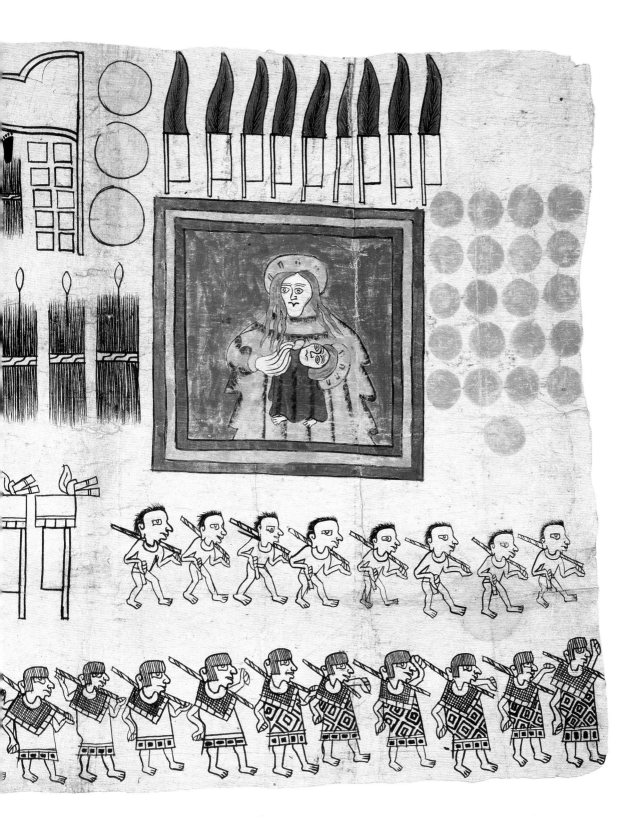

Founding
of the
Nation

James Madison's two volumes of notes on the debates in the Constitutional Convention of 1787 are the only complete, firsthand account of the secret sessions. Shown here is the first page of notes taken at the convention's opening session in Philadelphia, on 14 May 1787. Madison decided to preserve a record of the convention, because during his preparation for the sessions, he had been frustrated at the lack of documentation available on the formation of ancient confederacies. However, the convention's decision to keep its records a secret prevented Madison from publicizing his notes, and they were not printed until after his death in 1836. *(James Madison Papers)*

THE FOUNDERS OF THE UNITED STATES are not only those statesmen who installed our republican form of government but also the colonists who struggled to establish European settlements in the New World, the patriots who fought for American independence, and the pioneers who persistently expanded the country's boundaries. The experiences and contributions of all these founders are richly illustrated in the holdings of the Manuscript Division.

The records of the Virginia Company of London document some of the earliest contacts between European settlers and the Indians, whose complex civilizations in the Americas began centuries before. The military and diplomatic interaction between later generations of colonists and Native Americans may be researched in the papers of Andrew Jackson, James McHenry, Timothy Pickering, and the Return Jonathan Meigs family. Other holdings, like the Indian Language Collection and the papers of ethnologist Henry R. Schoolcraft, reflect more subtle and intellectual efforts of both civilizations to understand another. More than one hundred division collections focus on Native Americans and their part in the founding of the United States.

In 1898, within a year of its creation, the Manuscript Division acquired Benjamin Franklin Stevens's collection of facsimiles and transcripts of British manuscripts. Soon thereafter it obtained photoreproductions of additional papers relating to the founding of the Americas held in European archives. Donations from two private sources—James B. Wilbur in 1925 and John D. Rockefeller, Jr., in 1927—provided financial resources for the expansion of the division's Foreign Copying Program, which today has grown to include thousands of volumes of transcripts, photostats, microfiche, and microfilm. Although the main focus has been on manuscripts in British, French, and Spanish archives, materials have also been collected from Italy, Germany, the Netherlands, and Russia.

Supplementing the foreign reproductions were donations from two private collectors of original materials concerning the early Spanish and Portuguese explorations and settlements. The gifts of Edward S. Harkness in 1927 and Hans P. Kraus in 1969 have made available to the public invaluable documents for the first two centuries of European exploration, conquest, and settlement of the Americas. One document collected by Kraus is the manuscript "La Corónica Mexicana," written around 1600 by Fernando Alvarado Tezozómoc, a descendant of Aztec emperors, that traces the history of the Aztec empire before the arrival of Hernán Cortés. Letters of Amerigo Vespucci, whose name still graces the Americas, are another fascinating part of the Kraus legacy.

The papers assembled by Peter Force—a printer, mayor of Washington, D.C.,

1787

Monday May 14. was the day fixed for the meeting of the deputies in Convention for revising the federal system of Government. On that day a small number only assembled. Seven States were not convened till,

Friday 25 of May, when the following members appeared

Mr. Robert Morris informed the members assembled that by the instruction & in behalf, of the deputation of Pen.ᵃ he proposed George Washington Esqᵣ. late commander in chief for president of the Convention. Mr. Jn.º Rutledge seconded the motion; expressing his confidence that the choice would be unanimous, and observing that the presence of Genᵗ. Washington forbade any observations on the occasion which might otherwise be proper.

The General Washington was accordingly unanimously elected by ballot. and conducted to the chair by Mr. R. Morris and Mr. Rutledge; from which he thanked in a very emphatic manner, the Convention for the honor they had conferred on him, reminded them of the novelty of the scene of business on which he was to act, lamented his want of better qualifications, and claimed the indulgence of the House towards the involuntary errors which his inexperience might occasion.

[The nomination came with particular grace from Penn.ᵃ, as Doct. Franklin alone could have been thought of as a competitor. The Doct. was himself to have made the nomination of General Washington, but the state of the weather and of his health confined him to his house.]

Mr. Wilson moved that a Secretary be appointed, and nominated

Mr. Temple Franklin.
Col. Hamilton nominated Major Jackson.

On the ballot Major Jackson had 5 votes & Mr. Franklin 2 votes.
On reading the credentials of the deputies it was noticed that those from Delaware were prohibited from changing the article in the Confederation establishing an equality of votes among the States.
The appointment of a Committee consisting of Mr. Wythe, Hamilton &

C. Pinckney on the motion of Mr. Pinckney, to prepare rules, was the only remaining step of the day.

and publisher of the massive compilations *Documentary History of the American Revolution* and *The American Archives*—make up one of the division's most important collections relating to the founding of the nation. Force and his assistants toured the eastern United States in the early to mid-nineteenth century collecting original papers and transcripts about the settlement of the country and its Revolutionary period. Many of the original documents copied by them have now been lost to scholars and exist only in the transcripts held by the Library.

Force augmented his transcriptions with other people's collections. He acquired Ebenezer Hazard's newspaper, pamphlet, and manuscript collection relating to colonial and Revolutionary America, George Chalmers's British imperial documents, and Pierre E. Du Simitière's manuscripts relating to the American Revolution. He also transcribed large parts of the collections of Jeremy Belknap, Joseph Vallance Bevan, and William Buell Sprague. The Force collection includes documents as diverse as Native American papers relating to Anglo-Indian treaty negotiations; military papers of Revolutionary War heroes John Paul Jones and Nathanael Greene; accounts of Amsterdam merchant Jean de Neufville and London agent Joshua Johnson; and scientific correspondence, sketches, and other manuscripts of clergyman Jacob Cushing and steamboat inventor and craftsman John Fitch.

Other important collections of Americana, built by private individuals, are the papers of physician Joseph M. Toner (early medical and military records and Washingtoniana), Mary E. Powel (naval history), Hugh T. Taggart (early history of Maryland and the District of Columbia), John P. Morgan (signers of the Declaration of Independence), and J. Kelsey Burr, Jr. (Bank of the United States). The autograph collections of Sarah Stone, Henry A. Willard, and William Bebb also include letters and manuscripts of prominent early Americans, including the Revolutionary statesmen most often thought of as the nation's founding fathers.

Many of these leading founders are represented as well by their own collections of personal papers, which are vital to preserving and understanding our national heritage. Josiah Bartlett, the Pinckney family, Roger Sherman, Oliver Ellsworth, John James Beckley, the Breckinridge family, William Plumer, Elbridge Gerry, Gouverneur Morris, Robert Morris, and William C. Rives are just a few of the scores of founders whose papers are held in the Manuscript Division. To these must be added the papers of George Washington, Thomas Jefferson, James Madison, and James Monroe, whose founding roles culminated with their service as four of the nation's earliest chief executives.

The "Eastern Indians" and the governments of New Hampshire and Massachusetts signed this treaty at Portsmouth, New Hampshire, on 13 July 1713. The Indians' pictographic signatures are of particular interest to cultural historians. (*Levi Woodbury Papers*)

OPPOSITE. This plan for a fort is one of sixty-five thousand records of the Spanish administration of East Florida (1783–1821) which were seized by American officials in 1821 to prevent their removal to Cuba. In 1905 the records were transferred from Florida to the Library. (*East Florida Papers*)

Presidency

PRESIDENTIAL LIBRARIES ARE A FAMILIAR FEATURE of modern America. Since Herbert Hoover, presidents have been memorialized by library-museums that have preserved their papers and commemorated their achievements. Few people know that the Manuscript Division of the Library of Congress is the nation's oldest and most comprehensive presidential library, for while the recently built presidential libraries each hold the papers of a single chief executive, the Manuscript Division has in its custody the papers of twenty-three presidents, including the men who founded the nation, wrote its fundamental documents, and led it through the greatest crisis of its existence.

The Manuscript Division began acquiring presidential papers soon after the Library occupied the Thomas Jefferson Building in 1897. So imposing was the new structure that it seemed to be designed especially for the papers of a president. The new building was "the natural and fitting depository" for presidential papers, declared the descendants of Francis P. Blair, who in 1903 gave the division its first presidential collection, the papers of Andrew Jackson. Shortly after the Jackson Papers arrived, President Theodore Roosevelt signed the executive order transferring to the Manuscript Division the State Department's historical archives, which included the papers of George Washington, Thomas Jefferson, James Madison, and James Monroe. In the years after Roosevelt's order, the division assiduously acquired other presidential papers, obtaining some by purchase—the papers of James K. Polk and Andrew Johnson, for example—and many more by gift—those of Martin Van Buren, Grover Cleveland, William McKinley, Woodrow Wilson, and Calvin Coolidge, to name a few.

No gift was pursued with more patience and diligence than the papers of Abraham Lincoln. Librarian of Congress Herbert Putnam first approached the president's son, Robert Todd Lincoln, about the donation of his father's papers in 1901. Continued efforts to obtain the papers bore fruit in 1919 to the relief of all interested parties, for Robert had threatened to burn his father's papers and was apparently once interrupted in the act of doing so. He closed President Lincoln's papers to all researchers until twenty-one years after his own death, a step that produced a crop of rumors that the documents would reveal the complicity of the president's Cabinet in his assassination. The opening of the papers with great fanfare in 1947 dispelled the notion that they contained scandalous secrets.

The total number of items in the division's presidential collections exceeds two million. Collection size varies from a handful of documents, 631, in the Zachary Taylor Papers to the voluminous William Howard Taft Papers, 675,000

Theodore Roosevelt was a devoted father, who regularly wrote to his children when the family was apart. In this letter from ca. 1890, the future president entertains his young son Theodore with an illustrated fable about a wolf attacking a calf and about other barnyard animals rallying to drive the predator away. In addition to President Roosevelt's papers, the division holds the papers of three of his children: Theodore Roosevelt, Jr.; Kermit Roosevelt; and Alice Roosevelt Longworth. (*Theodore Roosevelt, Jr., Papers*)

A letter for Ted from his loving Father.

United States
Civil Service Commission,
Washington, D. C.

a cow, a calf, a pony and a big dog all lived very happily together in a barn yard in Texas

One day the cow and the calf walked out to the meadow, though the pony and the dog told them they had better not because there was a big wolf round

(I find the calf quite impossible to draw)

the wolf suddenly attacks them and tries to eat the calf, while the cow defends it.

Fortunately the pony has come trotting out and he looks over the hill & and sees what has happened

He runs back to tell the dog.

so they rush out and help the cow drive away the wolf and go back happily to the barn

Executive Mansion,

Washington, , 186 .

Four score and seven years ago our fathers brought forth, upon this continent, a new nation, conceived in liberty, and dedicated to the proposition that "all men are created equal"

Now we are engaged in a great civil war, testing whether that nation, or any nation so conceived, and so dedicated, can long endure. We are met on a great battle field of that war. We have come to dedicate a portion of it, as a final resting place for those who died here, that the nation might live. This we may, in all propriety do. But, in a larger sense, we can not dedicate—we can not consecrate—we can not hallow, this ground—The brave men, living and dead, who struggled here, have hallowed it, far above our poor power to add or detract. The world will little note, nor long remember what we say here; while it can never forget what they did here.

It is rather for us, the living, ~~to stand here,~~ we here be dedica-

ted to the great task remaining before us—that, from these honored dead we take increased devotion to that cause for which they here, gave the last full measure of devotion—that we here highly resolve these dead shall not have died in vain; that the nation, shall have a new birth of freedom, and that government of the people by the people for the people, shall not perish from the earth.

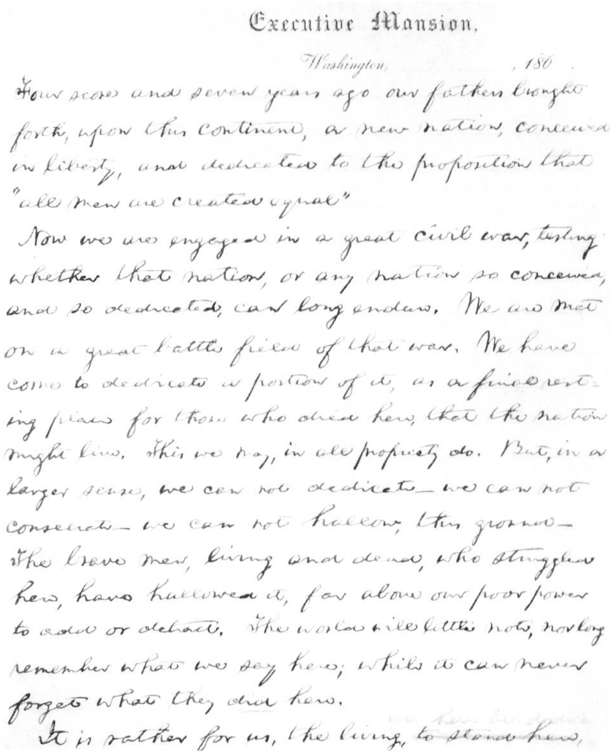

Seen here is the earliest extant version of Abraham Lincoln's Gettysburg Address. On 18 November 1863 Lincoln wrote the first page in ink at the White House on Executive Mansion stationery. He completed the second page in pencil at Gettysburg that evening or the following morning. This is the manuscript Lincoln used when he delivered his famous address. *(Abraham Lincoln Papers)*

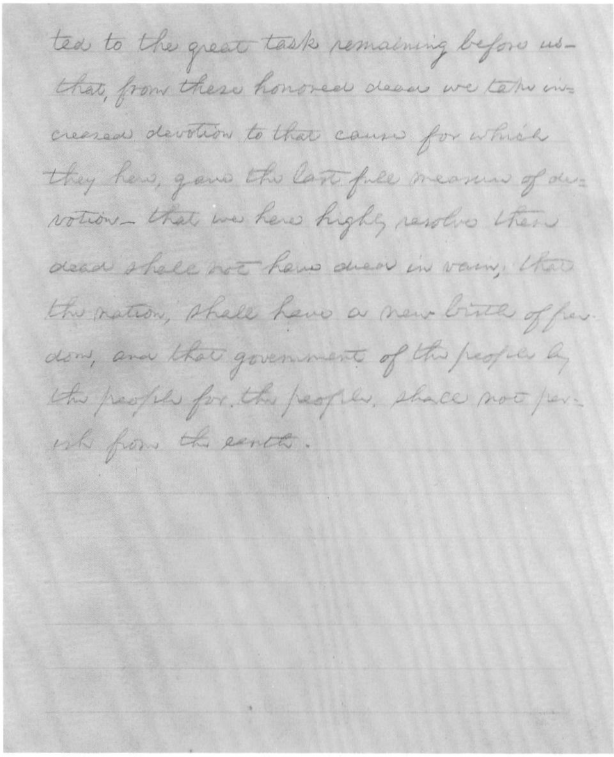

items. For those pre-presidential-library collections that the Manuscript Division does not have—the papers of John and John Quincy Adams, Millard Fillmore, James Buchanan, Rutherford B. Hayes, and Warren G. Harding—the division has obtained microfilm copies, with the result that scholars can consult in our reading room in one format or another a virtually unbroken line of papers from the administration of George Washington to that of Calvin Coolidge.

The presidential papers contain items that are among the most important individual manuscript treasures in the nation. In the Washington Papers are the father of the country's diaries, his commission as commander in chief of the American army, and his annotated copy of the United States Constitution. Jefferson's papers contain his rough draft of the Declaration of Independence with marginalia by Benjamin Franklin and John Adams. Madison's papers include the incomparable notes on the Constitutional Convention, the principal source for understanding the composition and meaning of the Constitution. In Lincoln's papers are the first draft of the Emancipation Proclamation, two drafts of the Gettysburg Address, and holograph copies of his first and second inaugural addresses. The Wilson Papers contain the original draft of the Fourteen Points.

So important to the nation are the division's presidential papers that Congress passed and President Dwight D. Eisenhower signed on 25 April 1958 an act to microfilm them and sell positive copies at cost to libraries around the nation. The Library's presidential papers can be consulted at dispersed, multiple sites, and in the event of a catastrophe, our national manuscript record shall not, in the words of one of its greatest creators, perish from this earth.

In a deep, low voice that betrayed what one observer called "manifest embarrassment," George Washington delivered his first inaugural address to Congress at Federal Hall, New York City, on 30 April 1789. (*George Washington Papers*)

21

III. In filling a blank with sums or time, the largest sum ~~& longest time~~ shall be first put to question. ~~the largest sum is privileged as a not smaller by the 18th rule of the Senate, contrary to the rule of parliament.~~ in filling blanks the longest time ~~but the 8th rule of Senate leaves it as privilege~~ is according to the rule of parliament. 2. Hats. 81.—83.

The Orders of the day are privileged by the law of parl. so that they may be called for to be read generally (but not a particular one) pending any question which is not an order of the day; and if it be carried to take them up, the orders must be proceeded on in the course in which they stand. 2. Hats. 81—83. 88. but the rule of the Senate has taken from the orders of the day all privilege against other questions.

IV. Another exception to the rule of priority is when a motion has been made to strike out a paragraph. the friends to the paragraph may make any amendments for rendering it as perfect as they can; which shall be put to the question before a vote is taken on striking out the whole paragraph. these amendments may be 1. by striking out. 2. by inserting words. 3. by substituting certain words for others, and here, if it be desired the question must be divided and put first on striking out, secondly on inserting. the paragraph as amended is then to be put to the question; the parliamentary form of which is 'Shall the paragraph [or words] stand part of it?' but the practice of the Senate is to put the question on striking out.

V. ~~The following is also an exception to the rule of priority. 2. Hats 81~~ But there are several questions which being incidental to every one, will take place of every one, privileged or not. these are

~~xxxxxxxxxxxxxxxxxxxxxxxxxxxxxxxxxxxxxxxxxxxxxxxxxxx~~
~~xxxxxxxxxxxxxxxxxxxxxxxxxxxxxxxxxxxxxxxxxxxxxxxxxxx~~

1. a question of order arising out of any other question, must be decided before that question. 2. Hats. 88.

2. a matter of privilege arising out of any question, or from a quarrel between two members, or any other cause, supersedes the consideration of the original question & must be first disposed of. 2. Hats. 88.

3. reading papers relative to the question before the house. this question must be put before the principal one. 2. Hats. 88. such a motion can only arise on a m. 2. or on an amendment. for it can scarcely be that there should be papers relating to the question of commitment, postponement, or the P. 2. these questions therefore could not be disturbed by a motion to read papers relative to them.

VI another exception against priority, is when a member wishes to withdraw his motion ~~if it is opposed to. a question must be put whether he~~ shall have leave, asked, to withdraw. ~~the then~~ the rule of parliament being that a motion moved & seconded is in possession of the house & cannot be withdrawn without leave; the very terms of the rule imply that leave may be given & consequently may be asked & put to the question. so determined by the chair Mar. 29. 98. on leave asked by mr Laurance to withdraw a motion & opposed by mr Anderson.

18
coexisting
questions

~~A question on~~ It may be asked whether the house can be in possession of two motions or propositions at the same time? so that one of them being decided, the other goes to question without being moved anew. the answer is that all of the class of privileged questions before enumerated may co-exist with their main question. but no other can. the rule being that when a motion has been made and seconded, no other can be received except it be a privileged one. the following decision therefore of the Sp. of the H. R. (mr Dayton) was erroneous. a motion had been made, & on that the P. 2. moved. the mover of the m. 2. wished to relieve the house by withdrawing his m. 2. but the Speaker decided that the m. 2. was no longer before the house, & therefore could

41798

Congress

As BEFITS THE LIBRARY OF CONGRESS, the papers of members of Congress also occupy a special place in its collections. More than nine hundred members are represented, from Patrick Henry and George Washington, delegates to the First Continental Congress in 1774, to John H. Glenn and Daniel P. Moynihan, members of the 102d Congress. The entire sweep of American history is covered in these collections, from the dawning of our independent political existence to the space age.

The course of the American Revolution and the creation of the nation that followed may be investigated in the papers of our earliest lawmakers, among them, Benjamin Franklin, Alexander Hamilton, Thomas Jefferson, James Madison, James McHenry, James Monroe, Gouverneur Morris, Robert Morris, and Roger Sherman. William Maclay, although less renowned, having served only two years (1789–91) as a senator from Pennsylvania, compiled a three-volume diary that chronicles the First Federal Congress; it is a classic document of the highest importance.

The papers of many senators and representatives reflect the formative roles they played in the great events before the Civil War. Their concerns included the War of 1812 and the war with Mexico, the Louisiana Purchase and territorial expansion that extended the nation's boundaries to the Pacific Ocean, the rise of an implacable slavery question, and the beginnings of a transportation and industrial revolution. Divisiveness attended all these issues and movements, leading to political, social, and economic upheaval that brought forth every shade of opinion in the halls of Congress. The papers of Henry Clay, Daniel Webster, and John C. Calhoun—the Great Triumvirate—are especially illuminating for this era. Other members, all later to be elected to the presidency and represented by collections of various sizes and complexion, include Andrew Jackson, Martin Van Buren, William Henry Harrison, John Tyler, James K. Polk, Franklin Pierce, James Buchanan, and Abraham Lincoln. Also contributing significantly to the understanding of these times are large collections of the papers of William Plumer, Samuel Smith, John J. Crittenden, William C. Rives, Levi Woodbury, Caleb Cushing, Thomas Ewing, James H. Hammond, Benjamin Tappan, Alexander H. Stephens, and Salmon P. Chase.

Just as the Civil War divided the nation, it tore apart Congress, with many southern seats staying vacant for several years after the war's end. The members who remained in Washington introduced and passed the legislation needed to raise armies, make the financial arrangements crucial to the war's prosecution, and cope with emergency situations as they arose. A special Joint Committee on

Thomas Jefferson wrote "A Manual of Parliamentary Practice" while he presided as vice-president over the Senate. This page is from his preliminary draft. First published in 1801, Jefferson's manual is still considered part of the rules of the House of Representatives. (*Thomas Jefferson Papers*)

Daniel Webster recorded here his opening remarks for his famous "Seventh of March" speech. Delivered in support of Henry Clay's Compromise of 1850, Webster's address is considered one of the most notable and controversial speeches ever delivered in the Senate. (*Daniel Webster Papers*)

the Conduct of the War was also formed. Its dominant members were Benjamin F. Wade, Thaddeus Stevens, and Zachariah Chandler, all of whose papers are in the Manuscript Division.

In the aftermath of the war, as the nation attempted to right itself, Congress faced problems involving the freed slaves, the formulation and passage of amendments affecting civil rights, the impeachment of Andrew Johnson, and the restoration of order in the South. Members whose papers illustrate the influential roles they played in clarifying and resolving these and related questions include Nathaniel P. Banks, James G. Blaine, Henry L. Dawes, William Pitt Fessenden, James A. Garfield, Justin S. Morrill, John Sherman, Benjamin F. Butler, Simon Cameron, John A. Logan, Elihu B. Washburne, Thomas F. Bayard, Joseph R. Hawley, and Carl Schurz. Some continued in office through the end of the century, acting on legislation concerned with monetary policies, the tariff, the rise of great corporations, labor, agriculture, immigration, and natural resources and were joined by other members—William McKinley, Benjamin Harrison, John Tyler Morgan, William M. Evarts, John Coit Spooner, William E. Chandler, Matthew S. Quay, Nelson W. Aldrich, and William Jennings Bryan—whose papers show how Congress contended with these matters.

The swift conclusion of the Spanish-American War toward the end of the nineteenth century dramatized the elevation of the United States to the status of

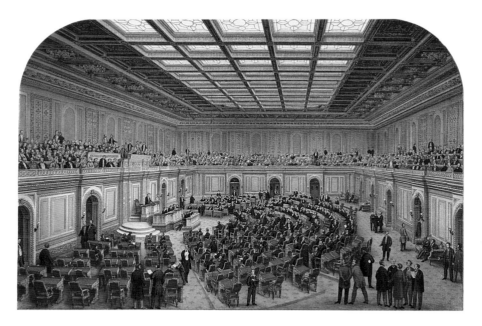

An 1866 lithograph by E. Sachse & Co. shows the "new" House of Representatives chamber, first occupied in December 1857 and still in use today. *(Prints and Photographs Division)*

a world power. Twentieth-century Congresses were required to meet the challenges of this new internationalism while also addressing increasingly complex domestic demands. Trust busting, regulatory legislation, conservation, the waging of a world war, and the making of peace are revealed in the papers of Albert J. Beveridge, John Sharp Williams, Victor Murdock, Nicholas Longworth, Elihu Root, Robert M. La Follette, and Thomas J. Walsh. George W. Norris and William E. Borah were noteworthy as long-term legislators whose papers extend from the early twentieth century into the era of the Great Depression, the New Deal, and the onset of World War II. Sharing in the legislative battles during the Franklin D. Roosevelt and Harry S. Truman administrations were Tom Connally, Emanuel Celler, Theodore Francis Green, Robert A. Taft, and James W. Wadsworth.

The papers of members of Congress clearly constitute an essential element in the ever-accumulating record of the American past. In recent times the character of these collections has changed considerably, notably in terms of size and completeness. Some of their intimacy may have been lost, however, as large congressional staffs necessarily assumed tasks and duties that a Daniel Webster would have undertaken himself, or with the help of a single secretary. Nevertheless, a member's papers will always possess that special character or quality that makes it possible to understand the individual and evaluate his or her work in the larger context of the ongoing legislative history of the United States.

Federal Judiciary

Chief Justice Earl Warren's brief 1955 opinion announcing the decree to enforce *Brown v. Board of Education,* decided one year earlier, held that school districts must eliminate racial discrimination "with all deliberate speed." Justice Felix Frankfurter had suggested the phrase and had used it in this draft of a memorandum prepared on 8 April 1955. It had been introduced into constitutional law by Justice Oliver Wendell Holmes, Jr., whom Frankfurter revered and whose graceful but later troublesome phrase had appeared in several Frankfurter opinions that had preceded Brown. *(Felix Frankfurter Papers)*

THE MANUSCRIPT DIVISION'S CONGRESSIONAL COLLECTIONS include the papers of many members who were instrumental in drafting legislation that shaped the character of the federal judiciary. Some of these legislators—James Madison and Oliver Ellsworth, for example—were architects of the federal judicial system by virtue of their roles in writing the Judiciary Act of 1789. In this century, special mention should be given to Congressman Emanuel Celler of New York and Senator Thomas J. Walsh of Montana, whose papers reflect their leading roles on congressional judiciary committees and their efforts to develop collegiality and cooperation among the branches of government. The extensive correspondence between Senator Walsh and many federal judges on modern procedural reform, for example, demonstrates the close working relationships required within government to make federal justice genuinely effective.

Papers relating to the executive branch also bear upon the federal judiciary, and the presidential papers described previously contain a wealth of material on judicial selection and nomination, the organization of courts, and the development of an agenda for federal criminal and civil litigation. Equally valuable for documenting the nation's judicial history are the many collections of papers of attorneys general from Edmund Randolph through Elliot Richardson as well as the papers of many solicitors general, including Benjamin Bristow, Charles Fahy, and Robert Bork, who argue the government's cases in the Supreme Court and in important litigation elsewhere.

The principal actors in the drama of federal justice, however, are the judges themselves. Here the division's collections are truly magisterial, for they include the nation's largest corpus of the papers of chief justices and associate justices, as well as those of many judges of the lower federal courts who played leading roles in American life. Among the chief justices, the division holds the papers of Oliver Ellsworth, John Marshall, Roger B. Taney, Salmon P. Chase, Morrison R. Waite, Melville Weston Fuller, William Howard Taft, Charles Evans Hughes, Harlan Fiske Stone, and Earl Warren. The papers of associate justices are also well represented here. For the Warren Court (1953–69) alone, the division holds the papers of Hugo L. Black, William O. Douglas, Felix Frankfurter, Harold H. Burton, Robert H. Jackson, William J. Brennan, Jr., Byron R. White, Thurgood Marshall, and Arthur J. Goldberg.

Judicial papers contain materials that range from diaries and family correspondence to scrapbooks of newspaper clippings. Although they are most useful for studying the development of law and government, the letters, opinions,

not refused admission to any school where they are situated
similarly to white students in respect to (1) distance from school,
(2) natural or manmade barriers or hazards, and (3) other relevant
educational criteria.

5. On remand, the defendant school districts shall be required
to submit with all appropriate speed proposals for compliance to
the respective lower courts.

6. Decrees in conformity with this decree shall be prepared
and issued forthwith by the lower courts. They may, when deemed by
them desirable for the more effective enforcement of this decree,
appoint masters to assist them.

7. Periodic compliance reports shall be presented by the
defendant school districts to the lower courts and, in due course,
transmitted by them to this Court, but the primary duty to insure
good faith compliance rests with the lower courts.

This mid-nineteenth-century photograph shows the Carroll Row boardinghouses, which were occupied by members of Congress and the justices of the Supreme Court between 1815 and 1835. The intimacy encouraged by such shared residential settings helped increase collegiality among the early justices and permitted opportunities to discuss and dispose of cases informally. Located on First Street between East Capitol and A Streets, S.E., the buildings were demolished in the winter of 1886–87 for construction of the Library of Congress Thomas Jefferson Building. *(Washingtoniana Collection, Prints and Photographs Division)*

and memoranda written by some justices, especially Frankfurter and Jackson, can stand on a shelf with the finest English prose.

The federal judiciary played a vanguard role in the modern civil rights movement. In addition to the papers of Supreme Court justices, the division also collects the papers of many lower-court judges, such as Simon E. Sobeloff, J. Skelly Wright, and Frank M. Johnson, Jr., who gave new meaning to basic constitutional guarantees. Modern federal judges have also played leading roles in the fields of administrative law, criminal justice, and legislative reapportionment, and these matters can be explored in the papers of Gerhard A. Gesell, Carl E. McGowan, Harold Leventhal, E. Barrett Prettyman, Clement F. Haynsworth, Jr., Shirley Hufstedler, Irving R. Kaufman, and Robert P. Patterson.

The papers of lawyers who practice in federal courts can also provide insights into judicial history, and among the most important are the papers of Daniel Webster, Moorfield Storey, Joseph H. Choate, Clarence S. Darrow, Elihu Root, Thomas G. Corcoran, James M. Landis, and Joseph L. Rauh, Jr. Modern litigation is often undertaken by public interest groups, and our understanding

of recent legal history is greatly enhanced by the records of the National Association for the Advancement of Colored People (NAACP), the NAACP Legal Defense and Educational Fund, and the Center for National Policy Review. Journalists who cover the federal judiciary have also placed papers in the division's care, helping scholars acquire an informed understanding of the judicial process from observers who are at once detached and engaged. Among the most important of these collections are the papers of Anthony Lewis and Fred P. Graham. The papers of journalists Joseph and Stewart Alsop are valuable for exploring as well such incidents as Franklin D. Roosevelt's court-packing plan, one of the most dramatic controversies in modern constitutional history. The research notes, memoranda, and interviews in the Alsop Papers are an exciting example of shoe-leather reporting at its best.

Throughout its many years of acquiring judicial collections, the Manuscript Division has been guided by Justice Byron R. White's challenge to gather materials for "a broadly conceived legal history ... directed toward the study of all legal institutions and to their interaction with the larger society.... "5

Joseph Keppler's cartoon, "Our Overworked Supreme Court," reflects the growth of the Court's docket from three hundred cases on the eve of the Civil War to more than thirteen hundred cases in 1885. Relief came six years later when Congress passed the circuit court of appeals act, which created the modern intermediate appellate court system. Of the justices represented in Keppler's cartoon, the Manuscript Division holds the papers of John Marshall Harlan and Morrison Remick Waite (*back row, third and sixth from the left*). Published in *Puck*, 9 December 1885. (*Prints and Photographs Division*)

Military Affairs

Located among President Andrew Jackson's papers is the former general's retrospective and fragmentary account of the Battle of New Orleans, the outstanding military event of the War of 1812. On the morning of 8 January 1815, the British attempt to take an entrenched American position was repulsed with great loss of life, and later that day, "a Bugal of the enemy was heard, & a white flag seen approaching our line—orders was given to the adgt. Genl to meet it in advance of the Piquet, & receive the communication— It was from Genl Lambert asking an armistice to bury his dead." Gen. John Lambert had assumed command of the British force after the death of Sir Edward Pakenham on the field of battle. His subsequent withdrawal permanently established the national image of Jackson as "The Hero of New Orleans." *(Andrew Jackson Papers)*

MILITARY RECORDS ARE ANOTHER IMPORTANT PART of the Manuscript Division's holdings. Included are the papers of military heroes from George Washington, commander in chief of the Continental Army, to Gen. Curtis E. LeMay, commanding general of the Strategic Air Command and chief of staff of the United States Air Force after World War II. Interspersed between these two luminaries are the collected or personal papers of numerous career officers, volunteers, and noncommissioned officers and enlisted personnel, as well as war correspondents, military spouses, camp followers, and private citizens caught in the path of war.

Our military collections span the entire history of the United States. They are particularly rich for the eighteenth and nineteenth centuries, and include several important collections relating to the British colonial wars, such as the diaries of Maj. Christopher French, a British officer who served in North America and the West Indies throughout the French and Indian War. In addition, the division has managed to acquire a significant amount of material from World Wars I and II, the Korean War, and the Vietnam War, even though many twentieth-century military papers have been deposited with one of the established or newly created war colleges or libraries.

Since few collections in the Manuscript Division bear the name of a particular war or military action, most of our patrons research military history through the careers of individual commanders and participants. The War of 1812, for example, is best represented in the papers of such individuals as Jacob J. Brown, William Henry Harrison, Andrew Jackson, Thomas Macdonough, James Madison, Duncan McArthur, Winfield Scott, and William H. Winder. The strength of the division's holdings on the Civil War is evident from the fact that it is the principal repository for the papers of President Abraham Lincoln as well as those of generals Nathaniel P. Banks, Pierre G. Beauregard, Benjamin F. Butler, Jubal A. Early, Richard S. Ewell, Charles Ewing, William B. Franklin, James A. Garfield, Ulysses S. Grant, Samuel P. Heintzelman, Henry J. Hunt, Joseph W. Keifer, George B. McClellan, Montgomery C. Meigs, Carl Schurz, Philip H. Sheridan, and William T. Sherman. Admirals Andrew Hill Foote, Louis M. Goldsborough, and Samuel Phillips Lee are also represented, as are hundreds of noncommissioned officers and enlisted personnel. The famous Confederate States of America collection, the papers of war correspondents Sylvanus Cadwallader *(New York Herald)* and Whitelaw Reid *(Cincinnati Gazette)*, and the papers of Burton N. Harrison, secretary to Jefferson Davis, are also among the more than one thousand collections in the division that relate to the Civil War.

the Detachment from the Kentucky Division had mounted 400 Strong—
The Brave ^(Genl) Humber was ordered to cross, & report himself for command to aid in the attack on the right Bank—
12 oclock in the day the 8th a Bugel of the enemy was heard, & a white flag seen approaching our line—orders was given to the Adjt Genl to meet it in advance of the Picquet, & receive the communication—It was from Genl Lambert asking an armistice to bury his dead—The communication was not signed as commander in—chief, & the commanding Genl thought it his duty to hold correspondence with none else, & replied to Genl—Lambert, to know whether he was then commanding in chief over the British forces—The Genl answered in the affirmative—The armistice was granted under certain condi:=tions for which see the official cor;=respondence—during 8th half past 3 O. oclock. P. M. Reported to the commandg Genl, that the rallied troops, with the reinforcements under Governor Clai borne were assembled near the

U. S. S. RANGER

NAVAL DISPATCH

Heading: NSS NR 977 Z 0F2 1830 0F3 0F4 0 BT

AIR RAID ON PEARL HARBOR X THIS IS NOT DRILL

EXECUTIVE

From: CINCPAC   Date 7 DEC 41 ED

To: CINCLANT CONAF OPNAV

Info:

A naval dispatch, received by the USS *Ranger*, reported the Japanese surprise attack on Pearl Harbor on 7 December 1941. The aircraft carrier *Ranger* was returning to Norfolk, Virginia, from an ocean patrol when the attack occurred. The dispatch is one of five thousand items in the papers of John J. Ballentine, aviator and naval officer, deposited in the division by the Naval Historical Foundation.

OPPOSITE. The Manuscript Division holds more than one thousand collections relating to the Civil War, including the papers of Gen. George B. McClellan, shown here with his wife, Mary Ellen Marcy McClellan. Signed carte-de-visite photograph taken in Philadelphia by F. Gutekunst, ca. 1864. (*James Wadsworth Papers*)

The papers of Gen. John Joseph (Black Jack) Pershing and Maj. Gen. John Archer Lejeune well document the role of the American Expeditionary Forces in World War I. For the World War II period, the division has the papers of generals Henry H. "Hap" Arnold, Ira C. Eaker, Curtis E. LeMay, and Carl A. Spaatz, who were instrumental in assuring Allied victory by establishing the United States as the world's greatest air power. The Edward L. Rowny Papers cover not only World War II but also the Korean and Vietnam wars and strategic arms negotiations on behalf of the North Atlantic Treaty Organization (NATO).

One of the chief sources of the division's naval collections has been the Naval Historical Foundation (NHF). The NHF collections contain in excess of 337,000 items under 254 separate titles and touch on naval affairs in the War of 1812, the Mexican War, the Civil War, the Spanish-American War, and World Wars I and II. Represented are such notables as Washington Irving Chambers, William Frederick Halsey, Stanford C. Hooper, and the famous Rodgers family. The papers of Adm. William Sowden Sims cover his service as commander of United States naval forces in Europe during World War I, and the papers of Adm. Ernest J. King relate primarily to his activities as commander in chief of the United States Fleet and chief of naval operations during World War II. Naval operations dur-

Lt. Col. John Paul Vann (*second from right*) briefs his colleagues in Vietnam. Vann served as an adviser to the South Vietnamese Army in 1962 and 1963. He believed that permanent American military success in Vietnam depended upon the creation of an effective native government. (*Vann-Sheehan Papers*)

OPPOSITE. Of the presidents whose papers are housed in the Library of Congress, Woodrow Wilson is one of five who fulfilled the duties of commander in chief during a major American war. Shown here is Wilson's pencil draft of his announcement of the armistice ending World War I on 11 November 1918. (*Woodrow Wilson Papers*)

ing the Vietnam War are highlighted in the papers of Adm. Edwin Bickford Hooper, Commander Service Force, United States Pacific Fleet.

Nor should presidential, congressional, or judicial collections be overlooked as primary sources for military historians. Of the presidents whose papers are housed in the Library, George Washington, William Henry Harrison, Andrew Jackson, Zachary Taylor, Ulysses S. Grant, James A. Garfield, and Theodore Roosevelt all had distinguished military careers before entering the political arena, and presidents James Madison, James K. Polk, Abraham Lincoln, William McKinley, and Woodrow Wilson each fulfilled the duties of commander in chief during a major American war. Many members of Congress also served in the military or were vocal in hearings and committees concerning the waging and financing of wars. Similarly, legal issues surrounding the wartime powers of presidents and the conduct of American military operations are reflected in several of the division's judicial collections. Consequently, given the breadth of the division's holdings, a scholar would be well advised to cast a wide net when searching for manuscript sources documenting the nation's military history.

My fellow countrymen, The armistice was signed this morning. Everything for which America fought has been accomplished. It will now be our fortunate duty to assist by example and by friendly sober counsel and by material aid in the establishment of just democracy throughout the world.

Woodrow Wilson

Foreign
Policy

Only the official records of the State Department surpass the richness of the Manuscript Division's holdings for documenting American foreign policy. The division houses the papers of more than half of the individuals who have served as secretary of state from the first secretary, Thomas Jefferson, who assumed office in 1789, to Alexander Haig, who resigned in 1982. More than two hundred other collections comprise the papers of diplomats or contain significant material relating to American diplomacy. These, too, span American history, from Benjamin Franklin's letters as the American colonies' diplomatic representative to France in 1776 to the papers of William Howard Taft IV, who became the United States ambassador to the North Atlantic Treaty Organization (NATO) in 1989.

The Manuscript Division also has the papers of some foreign diplomats whose careers illuminate aspects of American policy. "Citizen" Edmond Genet, the first ambassador of the French republic to the United States, is represented by a large collection of papers reflecting his turbulent, provocative, and spectacularly unsuccessful mission to this country. Genet's papers found their resting place in America, because the sanguinary politics of revolutionary France forced him to accept permanent exile in the United States, notwithstanding his feud with the American government.

Diplomacy during World War I is extensively documented in the division's holdings, notably in the papers of Robert Lansing. Of particular interest are nine volumes of private memoranda which Lansing started writing upon his appointment as secretary of state in 1915 and continued until after his resignation in 1920. These memoranda, which were kept confidential until 1949, include accounts of Cabinet meetings, detailed descriptions of the Paris Peace Conference, and vivid impressions of the dignitaries whom Lansing met. Twenty pages relate to the Cabinet meeting of 20 March 1917, which concerned America's entrance into the war, and another entire volume comprises a day-to-day account of the preparation of the Treaty of Versailles and of the covenant of the League of Nations.

In this century no foreign policy relationship has been so fraught with danger as that of the United States and the Soviet Union. The Library's manuscript resources are particularly rich for studying the relations between these two superpowers, as the division's holdings include the papers of several of this country's diplomats to tsarist Russia (including George Washington Campbell, Simon Cameron, and George von Lengerke Meyer) and five of its ambassadors to the Soviet Union (W. Averell Harriman, Charles E. Bohlen, Laurence A. Steinhardt, William H. Standley, and Joseph E. Davies). The Harriman Papers comprise one

This watercolor shows the temple in Macao where the first Sino-American treaty was signed in July 1844 clarifying the status of Americans in China and granting to the United States commercial privileges equal to those afforded to Great Britain. Drawn by George R. West, the item is in the papers of Caleb Cushing, the first American emissary to China, who negotiated the treaty.

Dear Sir   Monticello Oct. 24. 23.

The question presented by the letters you have sent me is the most momentous which has ever been offered to my contemplation since that of independance.
that made us a nation; this sets our compass, and points the course which we are
to steer thro' the ocean of time opening on our view. and never could we embark
on it under circumstances more auspicious. our first and fundamental maxim
should be, never to entangle ourselves in the broils of Europe; our 2d. never to suffer
Europe to intermeddle in Cis-Atlantic affairs. America, North & South, has a set
of interests distinct from those of Europe, and peculiarly her own. she should therefore have a system of her own, separate and apart from that of Europe. while the
last is laboring to become the domicil of despotism, our endeavor should surely be
to make our hemisphere that of freedom. one nation, most of all, could disturb us
in this pursuit; she now offers to lead, aid, and accompany us in it. by acceding
to her proposition, we detach her from the band of despots, bring her mighty
weight into the scale of free government, and emancipate at one stroke a
whole continent, which might otherwise linger long in doubt and difficulty.
Great Britain is the nation which can do us the most harm of any one, or all
on earth; and with her on our side we need not fear the whole world. with
her then we should the most sedulously nourish a cordial friendship; and
nothing would tend more to knit our affections than to be fighting once more
side by side in the same cause. not that I would purchase even her amity at the
price of taking part in her wars. but the war in which the present proposition might
engage us, should that be it's consequence, is not her war, but ours. it's object
is to introduce and to establish the American system, of keeping from our land all
foreign nations, of never permitting the powers of Europe to intermeddle with
the affairs of our nations. it is to maintain our own principle, not to depart from it.
and if, to facilitate this, we can effect a division in the body of the European powers,
and draw over to our side it's most powerful member, surely we should do it.
but I am clearly of mr Canning's opinion, that it will prevent war, instead

At the Moscow Conference in August 1942, W. Averell Harriman, President Franklin Roosevelt's special representative, met with Winston Churchill and Joseph Stalin to discuss the Soviet proposal for a second-front assault on Germany and alternative plans for Allied landings in North Africa. Interpreter V. Pavlov (*left*) and Soviet statesman Vyacheslav M. Molotov (*right*) are also pictured. (*W. Averell Harriman Papers*)

of the richest collections of primary source material on modern American foreign policy. Harriman served as director of Lend-Lease in Great Britain (1941–43), ambassador to the Soviet Union (1943–46), coordinator of the Marshall Plan (1948–50), United States negotiator for the Test Ban Treaty (1963), and American representative at the Paris peace talks with North Vietnam (1968–69). There is no better place to understand the development of the Cold War than in Harriman's papers, where one can follow the shift in his opinion from an initial view that American and Soviet goals were compatible to his 1945 warning that "the time has come for us to reorient our whole attitude and our methods of dealing with the Soviet government.... Unless we wish to accept the 20th Century barbarian invasion of Europe ... we must find ways to arrest the Soviet domineering policy."[6]

The Library's diplomatic collections are not limited to the papers of State Department officials and appointed ambassadors. Included as well are the papers of those who promoted the nation's foreign policy through covert means. For example, in a 1792 letter, David Humphreys, the American "minister resident" in Lisbon, Portugal, and a former aide-de-camp to George Washington, recommended to the American minister in Paris, Gouverneur Morris, that the United States assist the new revolutionary French government, then threatened with invasion by Austria and Prussia. Humphreys wrote, "If the Austrian & Prussian Armies should really enter France, they might be very much weakened & perhaps ruined by desertion, if suitable, secure & alluring measures could be taken to encourage it. Nothing, in my judgment, would be so likely to effect this, as for the Government of France to provide passages, at its own expense, for all such Non-Commissioned officers & Soldiers as should chose to go & settle in America."[7]

OPPOSITE. In this letter from Thomas Jefferson to James Monroe, dated 24 October 1823, the former president reacts strongly and positively to President Monroe's proposed doctrine forbidding European governments from establishing new colonies in the New World. Monroe had solicited advice from Jefferson, James Madison, and John Quincy Adams before announcing to Congress the doctrine which later bore his name. Jefferson's opening sentence sets the tone for what follows: "The question presented by the letters you have sent me is the most momentous which has ever been offered to my contemplation since that of independance [sic] that made us a nation; this sets our compass, and points the course which we are to steer thro' the ocean of time opening on our view." (*James Monroe Papers*)

WHITE HOUSE,
WASHINGTON.

July 1, 1902.

Personal.

My dear Mr. Secretary:

The great bit of work of my administration, and from the material and constructive standpoint one of the greatest bits of work that the twentieth century will see, is the Isthmian Canal. In the negotiations to start this straight I must trust to you and Knox. I hope you will take personal direction.

By the way, when you get the Cuban treaty back, of course Cullom and Hitt will have to be consulted about it.

Faithfully yours,

Theodore Roosevelt

Hon. John Hay,
    Secretary of State.

Humphreys's imaginative suggestion was not adopted, but "psychological warfare," as it came to be called, played a role later in American foreign policy. The papers of Central Intelligence Agency officials David Atlee Phillips, Archibald Roosevelt, Jr., and Cord Meyer document the institutionalization of American espionage and intelligence operations in the post-World War II period. These and other recently acquired collections focusing on the government's covert policies and activities complement the papers of ambassadors, members of Congress, and State Department officials who pursued more open and traditional diplomatic approaches to American foreign policy. When consulted together, the division's varied holdings provide a remarkably complete and nearly unparalleled record of this country's most significant foreign policy initiatives.

In 1946 Archibald Roosevelt, a United States intelligence officer, was one of the few Westerners to reach Mahabad, capital of a newly formed Kurdish republic. (*Archibald Roosevelt Papers*)

OPPOSITE. In this letter to John Hay, President Theodore Roosevelt instructed his secretary of state to oversee personally the negotiations to secure perpetual control of the Panama Canal. (*John Hay Papers*)

Arts and Literature

ALTHOUGH THE MANUSCRIPT DIVISION holds samples of the work of major European writers such as Shelley, Wilde, Shaw, and Ibsen, its greatest literary treasure consists of the papers of preeminent American poet Walt Whitman. Whitman's papers exemplify the rich literary flourishing—often called the American Renaissance—that began in the mid-nineteenth century and that also featured the writings of Herman Melville, Henry David Thoreau, Ralph Waldo Emerson, Mark Twain, and Emily Dickinson, all of whom are represented in the division's collections.

Whitman bequeathed his papers, books, and photographs to three literary heirs. The first, Thomas Harned, began donating his holdings to the Library of Congress in 1917. Thereafter, additions arrived from England and various corners of this country in support of Harned's idea of centralizing Whitman's papers in Washington. The large collection previously owned by Whitman's personal Boswell—Horace Traubel—came to the Library in 1980 through the renowned Whitman collector Charles Feinberg, who had donated his own vast Whitman collection in the 1970s. Today the division holds the world's most extensive collection of Whitman items, including the only surviving manuscript page from the first edition (1855) of *Leaves of Grass.* There are many drafts of Whitman's famous Lincoln lectures and poems, including the dirge "O Captain! My Captain!," which became so popular that the poet regretted writing it. Artifacts in the collection include Whitman's cane, spectacles, pen, watch, and the haversack in which he carried small gifts for wounded soldiers whom he visited in Washington area hospitals during the Civil War.

Twentieth-century literary papers include representatives of a wide array of movements, forms, and points of view. Those of western writers Owen Wister and Zane Grey reflect the popularity of local color writing at the turn of the century and of regional fiction in the 1920s and 1930s. The papers of Benjamin Holt Ticknor, Hiram Haydn, Oscar Williams, and Ken McCormick provide the perspective of literary agents and editors. Works by women range from those of the poet Muriel Rukeyser—who was concerned with the Spanish Civil War, women's rights, and the Vietnam War—to those of novelist-philosopher Ayn Rand—who championed individualism, capitalism, and anticommunism. Small but interesting collections exist for the poets Robert Frost, John Ciardi, and Louis Simpson. The division has a particular attachment to the papers of poet-dramatist Archibald MacLeish, who served as Librarian of Congress during World War II and reorganized the entire agency. The rich correspondence in MacLeish's papers include several outspoken letters from Ernest "Papa" Hem-

This early draft of Walt Whitman's "O Captain! My Captain!"—the famous dirge inspired by Abraham Lincoln's death—is one of the Manuscript Division's literary treasures. Whitman recited his popular poem and delivered his Lincoln lecture almost annually in the 1880s. Only two lines from this version of the much-revised poem survive in the final "deathbed" edition (1891–92) of the poet's lifetime verse compendium *Leaves of Grass. (Charles E. Feinberg–Walt Whitman Collection)*

My Captain

The mortal voyage over, the rocks and tempests pass'd,
The ship comes home again — the
The port is close, the bells we hear, the
As people all exulting,
While steady sails and enters straight the
wondrous veteran vessel;
But O heart! heart! heart! leave not
the little spot,
Where on the deck my Captain lies — cold
& dead.

O Captain! dearest Captain! wake up
& hear the bells;
Wake up & see the shining sun, & see the
flags a-flying;
For you it is the cities want — for you the
shores are crowded;
For you the red-rose garlands, and the electric eyes
of women;
O Captain! O my father! on arm I place
around you;
It is some dream that on the deck
You cold & dead.

The wondrous ship, the ship divine, that all

My captain does not answer, his lips
are closed & still,
My father does not feel my arm — he has
no pulse nor motion;
But the ship, I love is anchor'd safe — the
wondrous fearful trip over, and all
And the cities in triumph — but O
heart, heart,
Where on the deck my Captain lies, cold
& dead.

And cities
but my heart

And all career in triumph — but I with
gentle tread,
Walk the deck my captain lies, sleeps,
cold & dead.

The Hawaiian island of Kauai was the location for director Joshua Logan's 1958 blockbuster musical *South Pacific*, which was adapted from Logan's Pulitzer Prize-winning Broadway script. Actress Juanita Hall, shown here with Logan, recreated for the film her original stage role as Bloody Mary. (*Joshua Logan Papers*)

OPPOSITE. The germ of the idea for Bernard Malamud's short story "The Silver Crown" is seen in this 1971 *New York Times* clipping annotated by Malamud. The author's papers include notes, drafts, and galley proofs of his fiction. (*Bernard Malamud Papers*)

ingway about the incarceration of poet Ezra Pound for pro-Fascist war broadcasts from Italy.

Some of the modern fiction writers represented by major collections are James M. Cain, James A. Michener, Shirley Jackson, Bernard Malamud, Truman Capote, and Philip Roth. The original typescript of Cain's 1934 best-seller, *The Postman Always Rings Twice*, reveals the first title to have been *Bar-B-Q*. Prolific Michener's papers already number sixty thousand items, including photographs and diaries. The Jackson Papers feature drafts, adaptations, and information on the publishing history of her famous story, "The Lottery." Malamud's papers include a meticulous array of revisions valuable for textual study of his technique, Capote's papers feature notebooks for *In Cold Blood*, and Roth's papers include drafts and correspondence from his early career, best represented by *Goodbye Columbus*, through his 1993 *Operation Shylock*.

Theatrical papers have a long history in the division. Actress Frances "Fanny" Kemble caused a stir visiting the Capitol during highly oratorical pre-Civil War sessions, and some seventy-five items of her papers are here. A much larger collection documents the career of classical actress Charlotte Cushman. The John Thompson Ford Papers are a rich source for theatrical history from the manager's side, also providing interesting information on the assassination of President Abraham Lincoln at Ford's Theatre. Twentieth-century theatrical

Rabbi and 3 Indicted in Faith-Healing Case

By **MICHAEL T. KAUFMAN**

A 68-year-old Orthodox rabbi and three of his relatives were indicted in the Bronx yesterday on charges that they took money for cabalastic faith-healing rituals that never took place.

As unfolded by Burton B. Roberts, the Bronx District Attorney, the indictments told of people paying as much as $1,387 for health-restoring silver crowns that were never made. Others, the prosecutor said, financed prayers by "10 holy men" who, it was promised, would gather nightly for 26 consecutive nights to obtain cures for ailing supplicants. Mr. Roberts alleges that no "holy men" were assembled.

In four separate cases that have come to light so far, Mr. Roberts says, more than $5,000 was paid to the rabbi, Solomon Friedlander, who lives above his synagogue, the Congregation Herschel Lisker, at 2176 Grand Concourse.

On the basis of these cases the rabbi was indicted on charges of grand larceny. A second indictment charges the rabbi, his son, his son-in-law and a cousin with conspiring to steal money as faith healers.

Complaints From Rabbis

Mr. Roberts said his investigation began last spring when a number of rabbis came to his office, bringing with them members of their congregations who they charged had been gulled.

The complaints, Mr. Roberts said, came after April 6, when a television program on Channel 5 showed some people who declared that the rabbi's intercession had saved the lives of their loved ones.

A woman identified on the program as Mrs. Feldman said she had an 11-year-old daughter who had been critically ill with a rare blood disease, and who had miraculously been cured by the rabbi and was "dancing, running and laughing."

Mr. Roberts said that the wo-

Bronx Prosecutor Says They Did Not Provide Rituals They Took Money For

man in the interview had misrepresented her name — that she was actually the Rabbi's daughter, Mrs. Judith Friedlander. The prosecutor said that the child had indeed suffered from a blood disease, but that she had died three years before the TV program.

Publicity Grows

Articles about the rabbi began appearing in newspapers. One of these, Mr. Roberts said, was seen in Miami by a young man whose father was in a coma. The young man, who was identified only as a holder of a master's degree, visited the rabbi and asked that his father be saved from death.

According to the prosecutor, the supplicant was told to bring 401 silver dollars, which would be used to fashion a crown representing the health of his father.

In addition, he was allegedly told, the cost of making such a crown varied in proportion to how much the ailing person meant to the man pleading for his cure. Mr. Roberts said the applicant paid $986 for the most expensive crown.

The same young man, the prosecutor said, subsequently paid $500 more for the healing of a sick parakeet, which ultimately died.

The District Attorney said he had found that an average of almost 25 persons, "most of them old and ailing," would visit the synagogue for consultations on weekday afternoons. On Sundays, he said, there were close to 100. He said these included non-Jews.

Mr. Roberts appealed to any alleged victims to come forward now with their stories.

He said that a teacher suffering from asthma had complained to his office after giving $20 to the rabbi. A Jewish detective named Alan Bremmer was sent from Mr. Robert's office to accompany the woman, posing as her nephew.

The prosecutor would not specify Detective Bremmer's role, but credits him, in large part, with breaking the case.

Rabbi Friedlander pleaded not guilty before Supreme Court Justice Isidore Dollinger to both the grand larceny and conspiracy charges. His son, his son-in-law Rabbi Felix Friedlander, and a cousin, Jeno Friedlander, pleaded not guilty to conspiracy charges.

All were released in their own custody for a hearing Nov. 11. Rabbi Solomon Friedlander's daughter Judith and another cousin, Rabbi Moses Friedlander, were listed in the indictment as co-conspirators but not co-defendants.

A SHOTGUN BARREL PROVES POOR BANK

KERRVILLE, Tex. (UPI)—In a way, Creed Blevins, a Kerrville businessman, shot Santa Claus.

A few months ago he put a $100 bill in the barrel of keeping u
When ed, Mr. $100 bill and star Sever

membered his money. The idea for a moment was too monstrous to accept.

"I had to think for a minute whether I really did," he said. "I decided I to tell'

records include newer manifestations of the performing arts. Represented by major collections are film actress Lillian Gish; Broadway and Hollywood director Joshua Logan; television performer Sid Caesar; actor Vincent Price; humorist and actor Groucho Marx; and well-known theatrical couples Ruth Gordon and Garson Kanin and Jessica Tandy and Hume Cronyn.

The Library of Congress also holds some remarkable fine arts-related collections. American-born painter and etcher James A. McNeill Whistler is richly represented by a large collection compiled by Joseph and Elizabeth Robins Pennell, which includes drawings as well as correspondence and other manuscripts. Sculptors Paul Wayland Bartlett, John Gutzon de la Mothe Borglum, Jo Davidson, Daniel Chester French, Vinnie Ream Hoxie, Adelaide Johnson, Lee Oskar Lawrie, and William Zorach all have collections of papers in the Manuscript Division. Correspondence, client files, designs, drawings, photographs, and slides (divided among the Library's custodial divisions) document the influential career of industrial designer Raymond Loewy, who was responsible for the modern streamlined look of everything from the 1937 Pennsylvania Railroad S-1 locomotive and the 1947 Coca Cola dispenser to various "autos of the future" and the presidential aircraft, Air Force One.

The papers of photographer Frances Benjamin Johnston, celebrated chiefly for her portraits of prominent personalities, also include information on her photographs of southern gardens and architecture. Similarly, the papers of architects Montgomery C. Meigs, William Thornton, Charles Follen McKim, Frank Lloyd Wright, Ludwig Mies van der Rohe, and Howard Dearstyne document the design and construction of America's built environment, from bridges and aqueducts, to the United States Capitol, to award-winning modern commercial and residential structures.

Significant thinkers who interpreted the beliefs and behavior of the modern world are also represented in the division's collections, notably theologian Reinhold Niebuhr and philosopher Hannah Arendt. The papers of these conceptualizers, together with those of the artists and writers mentioned, provide a cultural picture of American civilization that will be represented, preserved, and reinterpreted in future generations.

Sculptor Daniel Chester French is shown in his studio working on a bust of industrialist Ambrose Swaysey, with a model of French's statue for the Lincoln Memorial in the background. Influenced by his years in Paris studying the Ecole des Beaux-Arts style, French gained fame for his allegorical heroic figures. (*Daniel Chester French Family Papers*)

My dear Mies:

Somebody has told me you were hurt by remarks of mine when I came to see your New York show. And I made them to you directly I think. But did I tell you how fine I thought your handling of your material was?

I am conscious only of two "cracks". One: you know you have frequently said you believe in "doing next to nothing" all down the line. Well, when I saw the enormous blow-ups the phrase "Much ado about your 'next to nothing'" came spontaneously from me.

Then I said the Barcelona Pavilion was your best contribution to the original "negation" and you seemed to be still back there where I was then.

This is probably what hurt (coming from me) and I wish I had taken you aside to say it to you privately because it does seem to me that the whole thing called "Modern-Architecture" has bogged down with the architects right there on that line. I didn't want to classify you with them - but the show struck me sharply as reactionary in that sense. I am fighting hard against it myself.

But this note is to say that I wouldn't want to hurt your feelings - even with the truth. You are the best of them all as an artist and a man.

You came to see me but once (and that was before you spoke English) many years ago. You never came since, though often invited.

So I had no chance to see or say what I said then and say now.

Why don't you come up sometime - unless the break is irreparable - and let's argue.

Affection,
Frank Lloyd Wright

October 25th, 1947

November 25th,
1947.

My dear Frank:

Thank you so much for your letter.

It was an exaggeration if you heard that my feelings were hurt by your remarks at my New York show.

If I had heard the crack " Much ado about next - to - nothing " I would have laughed with you. About " Negation " - I feel that you use this word for qualities that I find positive and essential.

It would be a pleasure to see you again sometime in Wisconsin and discuss this subject further.

As ever

Mr. Frank Lloyd Wright.
Taliesin.
Spring Green, Wisc.

This correspondence between architects Frank Lloyd Wright and Ludwig Mies van der Rohe concerns Mies's 1947 New York exhibition. Wright's letter and the draft of Mies's reply are in the Mies van der Rohe Papers. The division also holds a small collection of Wright Papers. Wright's letter, © 1972, is reproduced by permission of The Frank Lloyd Wright Foundation. Mies's reply is reproduced by permission of Georgia van der Rohe.

Science
and
Medicine

Alexander Graham Bell's notebook entry of 10 March 1876 describes his successful experiment with the telephone—speaking through the instrument to his assistant, Thomas A. Watson, in the next room. Bell wrote "I then shouted into M [the mouthpiece] the following sentence: 'Mr. Watson—come here—I want to see you.' To my delight he came and declared that he had heard and understood what I said." (*Alexander Graham Bell Family Papers*)

Over the years the manuscript division has acquired the papers of outstanding scientists, engineers, explorers, and inventors—collections that illustrate epochs of scientific endeavor ranging from Benjamin Franklin's path-breaking experiments in colonial America to Wernher Von Braun's contributions to space exploration. These collections offer glimpses of such diverse technological achievements as John Fitch's 1794 steamboat, John Ericsson's Civil War *Monitor*—the Union ironclad famous for its duel with the Confederate *Merrimac*—Samuel F. B. Morse's telegraph, Alexander Graham Bell's telephone, and Herman Hollerith's computer. Also documented are Margaret Mead's ethnographic studies of South Sea islanders, Sigmund Freud's analyses of human behavior, Gifford Pinchot's efforts to save American forests, Luther Burbank's plant breeding experiments, Frederick A. Cook's polar discoveries, J. Robert Oppenheimer's work on the atom bomb, and Gregory Pincus's development of the birth control pill.

Researchers can trace the history of communications in the Morse and Bell collections as well as in the papers of Lee De Forest. Morse's first telegraphic message with its stirring "What Hath God Wrought?" embossed in dots and dashes is among the Library's treasures. Bell's papers bear witness to his wide-ranging activities and multifaceted life; his laboratory notes contain early sketches of the telephone, and other papers reflect his interest in educating the deaf, eugenics, marine engineering, and aviation. Schematics and diagrams are among the papers of De Forest, inventor of the vacuum tube and other electronic devices essential to the development of radio.

The archives of the American Institute of Aeronautics and Astronautics contain photographs and other materials spanning the history of aviation from Thaddeus Lowe's Civil War ballooning exploits to modern space rocketry. These archives supplement the personal papers of Wilbur and Orville Wright, whose notebooks and diaries cover the brothers' scientific experiments as well as their celebrated flights at Kitty Hawk, North Carolina. Orville's entry for 17 December 1903, describing the first successful powered flight, recreates a remarkable moment in aviation history.

Of the Library's strong psychoanalytical collections, the papers of Sigmund Freud, written in his unique gothic script, are by far the most significant. In addition to his correspondence with other practitioners and members of his family, the Library holds manuscripts of many of his monographs and of one of his most famous cases, that of Sergius Pankejeff—"the Wolf-Man." Complementing this file are Pankejeff's own papers, which include many of his paint-

March 10th 1876

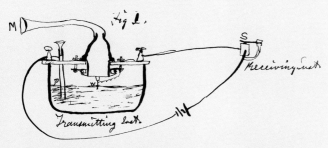

Fig. I.

M

S

Receiving Inst.

P   W

Transmitting Inst.

1. The improved instrument shown in Fig. I was constructed this morning and tried this evening.

P is a brass pipe and W the platinum wire M the mouth piece — and S the armature of the Receiving Instrument.

Mr Watson was stationed in one room with the Receiving Instrument. He pressed one ear closely against S and closed his other ear with his hand. The Transmitting Instrument was placed in another room and the doors of both rooms were closed.

I then shouted into M the following sentence: "Mr Watson — Come here — I want to

see you"   To my delight he came and declared that he had heard and understood what I said.

I asked him to repeat the words — He answered "You said 'Mr Watson — come here — I want to see you'."   We then changed places and I listened at S while Mr Watson read a few passages from a book into the mouth piece M.   It was certainly the case that articulate sounds proceeded from S. The effect was loud but indistinct and muffled.

If I had read beforehand the passage given by Mr Watson I should have recognized every word.   As it was I could not make out the sense — but an occasional word here and there was quite distinct. I made out "to" and "out" and "further"; and finally the sentence "Mr Bell Do you understand what I say? DO—YOU—UN—DER—STAND—WHAT—I—SAY" came quite clearly and intelligibly.   No sound was audible when the armature S was removed.

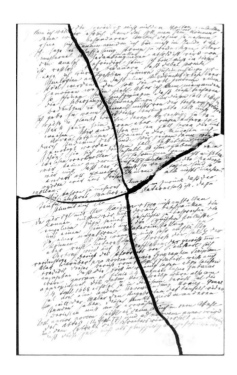

Scholars are grateful to whoever rescued the discarded pages of Sigmund Freud's draft of "Eine Teufelsneurose im siebzehnten Jahrhundert" ("A Seventeenth-Century Demonological Neurosis"), which differ from the final published version. (*Sigmund Freud Collection*)

OPPOSITE. Margaret Mead and her husband Gregory Bateson are shown doing field research in Papua, New Guinea, in 1938. This landmark research expedition, which began and ended in Bali, Indonesia, was the first to use photography to document native cultures. (*Margaret Mead Papers*)

ings and drawings, and the papers of Pankejeff's analyst, editor, and friend Muriel Gardiner.

Insight into the history of nineteenth-century medical practice may be found in the Joseph M. Toner Papers. Similarly, the papers of Abraham Flexner, who studied American medical schools at the beginning of the twentieth century, are of major importance, since they provided the basis for his controversial report *Medical Education in the United States and Canada* (1910), which revolutionized the teaching of medicine and forced more than half of the existing schools to close.

The extensive papers of anthropologist Margaret Mead include the "Pacific Ethnographic Archives," a mass of field notes, diaries, and oral transcripts assembled by Mead and her associates. Production materials document most of Mead's writings, and the rich photographic files testify to her pioneering application of that technique to anthropology. Nearly ninety years before Mead's first field trip to Samoa, Charles Wilkes commanded a navy expedition (1838–42) to the northwest coast of the United States, the Antarctic, and the Pacific islands. His papers include diaries, maps, and notebooks containing a wealth of scientific information. The recent acquisition of the Frederick A. Cook Papers refocuses attention on the enduring controversy over who was the first person to reach the North Pole—Cook or Adm. Robert E. Peary.

Beginning with the Second World War, an increasingly close relationship has developed between government and the scientific community. A vast amount of federal money has been spent on sponsored research, much of it concentrated on the development of atomic energy, a story well told in the division's collections. The papers of Vannevar Bush, a prime mobilizer of the scientific community, document his role as director of the Office of Scientific Research and Development (OSRD) and supervisor of the Manhattan Project, which developed the atom bomb. Complementing the Bush Papers are those of J. Robert Oppenheimer, head of the Los Alamos atomic project. Oppenheimer remained a key figure in atomic policy matters until his security clearance was revoked in a controversial action in 1954, a subject that coincidentally is recorded in the papers of journalists Joseph and Stewart Alsop, two of Oppenheimer's staunchest defenders. Closely associated with Oppenheimer was I. I. Rabi, a leading molecular physicist and scientific statesman, whose papers document his participation on many government advisory committees and his contacts with the international scientific community.

Commanding public attention today are questions about the fate of the

William Hornaday, a leading naturalist and longtime crusader for wildlife conservation, was photographed here in 1920 feeding one of his charges in the New York Zoological Park (popularly called the Bronx Zoo because of its location). Hornaday, the park's founding director, sought to use its "natural" surroundings to establish breeding populations of vanishing animals. *(William T. Hornaday Papers)*

OPPOSITE. In this 1795 handbill, John Fitch announced the invention of his steamboat and sought funds to perfect his machine. Though Fitch built boats that successfully hauled passengers, they were commercial failures. *(Peter Force Collection)*

earth. Several of the division's collections concern this subject. The conservation manifestos and other papers of William Hornaday, longtime director of the New York Zoological Park, reveal his efforts to preserve native animals, particularly a remnant herd of American bison. The papers of Barry Commoner, the "Paul Revere of environmental activists," speak to contemporary concerns about ecology, and the papers of Pulitzer Prize-winning biologist and environmentalist E. O. Wilson reflect his impassioned and sometimes controversial discussions of biodiversity.

To the ENCOURAGERS of

Useful Arts.

THE subscriber humbly begs leave to inform the Public, that he has proposed a MACHINE for the improvement of NAVIGATION, with other useful ARTS—That it has been honored with the Approbation of many men of the first characters for philosophical and mechanical knowledge in each of the middle states—That he has laid it before the honorable Assembly of Pennsylvania now sitting, whose committee have been pleased to make a very favorable report on the subject.   The result has been,—that a number of gentlemen of character and influence have undertaken to promote a subscription for his MAP of the N. W. parts of the United States, in order to enable him to make a full experiment of said Machine.   He flatters himself the subscribers will think the Maps well worth the money, yet he pledges himself to employ one half of the money so contributed, in constructing and bringing to perfection a Machine that promises to be of infinite advantage to the United States.   JOHN FITCH.

N. B. The following opinion was given to said Fitch, and subscribed by a number of gentlemen whose names would do honor to any projection in philosophy or mechanism.—

UPON considering the extent of the principles on which Mr. Fitch proposes to construct his STEAM-BOAT, and the quantity of motion that may be produced by the elastic force of steam, we are of opinion, that if the execution could by any means be made to answer the theory when reduced to practice, it might be beneficial to the public, and it seems to be deserving of a fair experiment, which alone can justify the expectation of success.   *Dec.* 20, 1785.

Subscriptions taken in by

Philadelphia: Printed by DUNLAP & CLAYPOOLE, *in Market-street, near the Court-House.*

African-American History and Culture

Abraham Lincoln's preliminary draft of the Emancipation Proclamation was shown to his Cabinet in July 1862. In it, Lincoln warns that if the rebellion is not ended in four months, as a "necessary military measure" he will "order and declare . . . all persons held as slaves within any state or states, wherein the constitutional authority of the United States shall not be practically recognized, submitted to, and maintained, shall then, thenceforward, and forever be free." *(Abraham Lincoln Papers)*

THE MANUSCRIPT DIVISION has one of the nation's most valuable collections for the study of African-American history and culture. The Library's holdings include information about slavery and the slave trade as well as other aspects of plantation life. Papers of slaveholders provide one view of slavery, and slave narratives give another. Diaries and journals further illuminate lives spent in slavery and freedom. The manuscripts of black and white abolitionists such as Frederick Douglass and Salmon P. Chase describe the efforts of those who attempted to alleviate the plight of slaves, and the records of the American Colonization Society detail the saga of African Americans who left the United States and established the West African nation of Liberia in the mid-nineteenth century. Papers relating to black participation and victimization in the Civil War abound, and African-American history during Reconstruction is reflected in collections pertaining to newly elected black officials such as John Mercer Langston, Blanche K. Bruce, Hiram R. Revels, and Francis L. Cardozo.

Efforts by African Americans to educate themselves and find meaningful employment can be traced in the papers of historian Carter G. Woodson and educator Nannie Helen Burroughs. Also available are the papers of the first three presidents of Tuskegee Institute—Booker T. Washington, Robert Russa Moton, and Frederick D. Patterson. The papers of Gen. Noel F. Parrish—the white World War II commander of the Tuskegee air base where black airmen were trained by the army air corps for the first time—reveal how blacks and whites worked together to dispel racist presumptions of black inferiority. Information on the training of black aviators and the establishment of the Tuskegee flight school may also be found in the diaries of historian Rayford W. Logan, who in the early 1940s was acting chair of the Committee on Participation of Negroes in the National Defense Program.

Logan is best known as a historian and professor at Howard University, but like other prominent black educators he was also involved in civil rights activities. The papers of historian Lorenzo J. Greene, who taught for many years at Lincoln University in Missouri, similarly reflect his involvement in the National Urban League (NUL) and the National Association for the Advancement of Colored People (NAACP), his participation on two different presidential commissions concerning the status of blacks and children, and his authorship of an important study on school desegregation for the United States Civil Rights Commission. The papers of Kenneth Bancroft Clark also reveal a college professor and social psychologist whose concern with the psychology of racism brought him national attention in the post-World War II era, when his research

In pursuance of the sixth section of the act of congress entitled "An act to suppress insurrection and to punish treason and rebellion, to seize and confiscate property of rebels, and for other purposes" Approved July 17. 1862, and which act, and the joint Resolution explanatory thereof, are herewith published, I, Abraham Lincoln, President of the United States, do hereby proclaim to, and warn all persons within the contemplation of said sixth section to cease participating in, aiding, countenancing, or abetting the existing rebellion, or any rebellion against the government of the United States, and to return to their proper allegiance to the United States, on pain of the forfeitures and seizures, as within and by said sixth section provided —

And I hereby make known that it is my purpose, upon the next meeting of Congress, to again recommend the adoption of a practical measure for tendering pecuniary aid to the free choice or rejection, of any and all States, which may then be recognizing and practically sustaining the authority of the United States, and which may then have voluntarily adopted, or thereafter may voluntarily adopt, gradual abolishment of slavery within such State or States — that the object is to practically restore, thenceforward to be maintain, the constitutional relation between the general government, and each, and all the States, wherein that relation is now suspended, or disturbed; and that, for this object, the war, as it has been, will be, prosecuted. And, as a fit and necessary military measure for effecting this object, I, as Commander-in-Chief of the Army and Navy of the United States, do order and declare that on the first day of January, in the year of our Lord one thousand, eight hundred and sixty three, all persons held as slaves within any state or states, wherein the constitutional authority of the United States shall not then be practically recognized, submitted to, and maintained, shall then, thenceforward, and forever, be free.

17233

on the detrimental effects of segregation was cited in the 1954 Supreme Court decision *Brown v. Board of Education of Topeka, Kansas.*

The division's collections are particularly strong for the history of the twentieth-century civil rights movement. The work of individual activists, rights organizations, and jurists is well represented. The NAACP and the NUL were founded in the first decade of the twentieth century and became important vehicles for the advancement of civil rights for blacks in the United States. Both, in turn, selected the Library of Congress as the repository for their records. While the NUL has tended to concentrate its efforts in the area of equal employment opportunities for blacks, the NAACP has moved forward on many fronts and has been most successful in its drive for equal legal protection. The NAACP led the struggle for the abolition of segregation, discrimination, lynching, and other forms of racial oppression.

The NAACP headquarters and Washington bureau records include more than two million items, which provide a rich source for the social history of black Americans in the twentieth century. In addition to these organizational records, the division holds the personal papers of some of the individuals who worked closely with the NAACP such as Moorfield Storey, the association's first president; Arthur B. Spingarn, its third president; and Roy Wilkins, longtime administrator and executive director from 1965 to 1977. The division also holds the records of the NAACP Legal Defense and Educational Fund, which was created by the NAACP just before World War II but eventually became independent of the parent organization. The fund's records document its presence at the forefront of the legal struggle for civil rights. Complementing these records are the personal papers of Justice Thurgood Marshall, who was the special counsel and director of the fund from its creation until 1961, when President John F. Kennedy appointed him to the United States Court of Appeals for the Second Circuit.

Other important civil rights activists and organizations represented in the Manuscript Division include the Brotherhood of Sleeping Car Porters, whose records date from 1920 to 1968, and the union's founder, Asa Philip Randolph, who also served as its president from 1925 to 1968. The papers of Bayard T. Rustin, a close associate of Randolph and an apostle of non-violent action, are also in the division's holdings.

The papers of two well-known political figures, Patricia Roberts Harris and Senator Edward W. Brooke, illustrate the efforts of African Americans to move into the center of the political arena. Harris, the first black woman to hold a Cabinet position, served as secretary of housing and urban development and sec-

This manuscript (ca. 1891) of an autobiographical article is in the hand of Frederick Douglass, who prepared it for *The National Cyclopedia of American Biography.* Douglass was born a slave in Talbot County, Maryland, but escaped in 1838 and eventually became a renowned abolitionist, orator, journalist, and public official. In 1845 he published a full-length autobiography and subsequently produced two revised versions. Drafts of these are among his papers held in the Manuscript Division. *(Frederick Douglass Papers)*

This photograph of former slave Lucindy Lawrence Jurdon accompanied the transcript of an oral history interview conducted with her during the 1930s as part of the ex-slave narrative program of the Work Projects Administration's Federal Writers Project. In seventeen states WPA workers interviewed hundreds of African Americans born before the passage of the Thirteenth Amendment outlawing slavery in 1865. Some of the informants were infants and small children when the Civil War ended, but others were old enough to have experienced and remembered many aspects of slavery. The narratives often are as interesting to historians studying the history of African Americans in the 1930s as to scholars examining the antebellum period. *(United States Work Projects Administration, Federal Writers Project Records)*

retary of health, education, and welfare (later called health and human services) under President Jimmy Carter. Brooke was the third black United States senator in the nation's history and the only one elected in this century until Carol Moseley Braun's recent victory.

The division's African-American manuscript collections have served historians well, supporting the much-increased scholarship in black history that began in the 1960s. The NAACP records are annually the most heavily used collection in the division, and other black history collections attract large numbers of scholars, testifying to their importance not only to the Library but to the nation itself.

Appearing in the forefront of this photograph of the 1963 March on Washington for Jobs and Freedom are Joseph L. Rauh, Jr., Washington lawyer and civil rights activist; Whitney M. Young, Jr., executive director of the National Urban League (NUL); Roy Wilkins of the National Association for the Advancement of Colored People (NAACP); A. Philip Randolph, founder and head of the Brotherhood of Sleeping Car Porters; and Walter Reuther, president of the United Automobile Workers Union of America (UAW). March participants called on President John F. Kennedy and the Congress to enfranchise African Americans, and give them equal access to public facilities, quality education, adequate employment, and decent housing. Among the division's unparalleled sources for the study of the twentieth-century civil rights movement are the personal papers of Rauh, Wilkins, and Randolph, as well as the organizational records of the NAACP, the NUL, and the Brotherhood of Sleeping Car Porters. *(Prints and Photographs Division)*

THE NEW EMPHASIS ON SOCIAL HISTORY in the late 1960s and early 1970s not only led to an increased awareness of African-American history but also promoted greater scholarly interest in the history of women. Fortunately, the curators of the Library's manuscript holdings at the beginning of the twentieth century had the foresight to assemble one of the nation's best collections for the study of women's experience in America.

In 1903, the same year that President Roosevelt directed the transfer of presidential papers and historical manuscripts from the State Department, Librarian of Congress Ainsworth Rand Spofford acquired the personal library and manuscripts of his friend Susan B. Anthony. Accompanying Anthony's papers were four portfolios of documents from her mentor, Elizabeth Cady Stanton, one of the founders of the women's rights movement. These included a manuscript copy of Stanton's controversial best-seller, *The Woman's Bible* (1895), which—to the horror of many suffragists—criticized church authority and attacked the use of Scripture to promote women's subjugation. Throughout the next half-century, the Manuscript Division augmented the Stanton and Anthony collections with the papers of other prominent suffragists—notably Carrie Chapman Catt and the Blackwell family—amassing in the process an unparalleled source of documents relating to American women's fight for the vote. The division supplemented the papers of individual suffragists with the records of two significant organizations, the National American Woman Suffrage Association (NAWSA) and its more militant offshoot, the National Woman's Party (NWP). Once suffrage was secured, the NAWSA regrouped as the League of Women Voters (LWV), whose records are also held by the division. The league, which initially worked with the NWP on a variety of women's and family issues, split with the more radical group over the NWP's campaign for the Equal Rights Amendment (ERA), drafted by Alice Paul in 1923. Scholars researching the league's position also benefit from having at the Library the records of the Women's Joint Congressional Committee (WJCC), an umbrella organization of approximately ten women's and social reform groups, which resisted the ERA as a threat to the protective labor legislation that its members had fought for years to secure. Other documentation on the long and ultimately unsuccessful campaign for an equal rights amendment may be found in the division's numerous congressional collections and the records of ERAmerica, a nationwide alliance of more than 130 civic, labor, church, and women's organizations founded in 1976 to promote ratification of the amendment that had passed Congress in 1972.

Many of the early suffragists came to the movement by way of the aboli-

Women's long and difficult struggle for suffrage is well documented in the Manuscript Division's collections. The records of the National American Woman Suffrage Association (NAWSA) and the National Woman's Party (NWP) show that suffrage was achieved only after the NAWSA abandoned its emphasis on state legislation and joined the NWP in a push for a federal amendment, combining the NAWSA's low-key lobbying of Congress with the NWP's use of militant shock tactics and pickets directed against President Woodrow Wilson, like the one shown here before the White House in January 1917. *(Records of the National Woman's Party, Group II)*

The diaries of Anna Maria Thornton, wife of architect William Thornton, are an invaluable source of information about Washington from 1793 to 1860. On 24 August 1814, Thornton wrote of the British occupation of the city and the retreating army's efforts to safeguard "Gen'l. Washington's picture & a cart load of goods from the president's house...." (*Anna Maria Thornton Diaries*)

OPPOSITE. A self-portrait of photographer Frances Benjamin Johnston shows her in her studio, about 1896. The cigarette, beer stein, and exposed petticoat symbolized rebellion against traditional ideas of feminine behavior. Johnston's papers are in the Manuscript Division, and her photographs, including this one, are in the Prints and Photographs Division.

tionist cause; in their struggle to free the slaves, they became more aware of their own secondary status. The division's collections of Julia Ward Howe and Anna E. Dickinson papers are excellent sources for understanding women's involvement in the antislavery movement and the adoption of techniques and strategies from that struggle for use in the woman suffrage campaign.

After women secured the right to vote, many former suffragists and their daughters became active in a variety of other reform initiatives, including advocacy of child-labor and child-abuse legislation, world peace, birth control, civil rights of minorities and women, conservation of natural resources, workplace safety, hour-and-wage legislation, fair labor standards, and consumer issues such as pure-food-and-drug legislation. The papers of Belle Case La Follette, Cornelia Bryce Pinchot, Sophonisba Breckinridge, Mary Church Terrell, and Margaret Sanger provide superb examples of women's twentieth-century reform impulse. Collections of personal papers are supplemented by large and extensive organizational records of the National Women's Trade Union League (NWTUL), National Consumers League (NCL), National Association for the Advancement of Colored People (NAACP), National Council of Jewish Women (NCJW), and Child Labor Committee.

In addition to documenting women's political activities, the division's holdings also serve historians attentive to women's everyday existence and the ways in which gender has shaped cultural affairs and domestic politics in the United States. The papers of Elizabeth Shaw, Mercy Otis Warren, Dolley Madison, Anna Maria Thornton, Issa Desha Breckinridge, Edith Bolling Wilson, Evalyn Walsh McLean, and the unknown female relatives corresponding with the hundreds of male politicians, soldiers, and sailors represented in the division's collections reflect the daily activities, concerns, and observations of American women from the colonial period through the twentieth century. Many of these women were less involved in reform crusades than in the daily struggle of existing in a society that devalued their contributions and restricted their activities. Their lives are recorded, if only because their papers often arrived in the division with the papers of a more famous husband, father, or brother.

Women's labor outside the home is also well documented, especially for the literate white middle class. Nineteenth-century work as missionary, teacher, and nurse is represented, for example, by the papers of Fidelia Church Coan, Myrtilla Miner, and Clara Barton. More recent collections reflect the expansion of women's employment opportunities in the twentieth century. Included, among others, are the papers of government officials Clare Boothe Luce, Ruth Hanna McCormick, Katie S. Louchheim, Shirley Hufstedler, and Patricia Roberts Harris. Actresses Lillian Gish, Margaret Webster, and Ruth Gordon, aviator Marjorie Claire Stinson, and authors Shirley Jackson and Edna St. Vincent Millay are also represented. Moreover, diplomat Florence Jaffray Harriman, judges Florence E. Allen and Sandra Day O'Connor, and journalists Ruby Aurora Black, Bess Furman, Elisabeth May Craig, and Ethel L. Payne all have papers in the Manuscript Division.

Spanning all time periods, classes, races, and occupations, the Library's sources for the study of women's history are among the finest and most comprehensive anywhere. Contained in nearly every collection are materials of interest to women's historians reflecting the full range of women's experiences, from Abigail Adams's declaration to her sister in 1799 that she would "never consent to have our sex considered in a inferior point of light"[8] to the remarks of Patricia Roberts Harris, "the daughter of a dining car porter" who told a skeptical senator at her 1977 confirmation hearing, "If my life has any meaning at all, it is that those who start out as outcasts can wind up being part of the system."[9]

Notes

1. Thomas Jefferson to Hugh P. Taylor, 4 October 1823, Thomas Jefferson Papers, Manuscript Division, Library of Congress.

2. Carl Sandburg, *Lincoln Collector: The Story of Oliver R. Barrett's Great Private Collection* (New York: Harcourt, Brace and Company, 1949), 4.

3. James Madison to John G. Jackson, 27 December 1821, James Madison Papers, Manuscript Division, Library of Congress.

4. Dolley Madison to Mrs. Andrew Stevenson, 1826, as quoted in Allen C. Clark, *Life and Letters of Dolly Madison* (Washington: W. F. Roberts Co., 1914), 223.

5. Byron R. White, "Introduction," in *Law in American History*, ed. Donald Fleming and Bernard Bailyn (Boston: Little, Brown and Company, 1971), xi.

6. W. Averell Harriman cable to State Department, 21 March 1945, W. Averell Harriman Papers, Manuscript Division, Library of Congress.

7. David Humphreys to Gouvernor Morris, 17 August 1792, David Humphreys Papers, Miscellaneous Manuscripts Collection, Manuscript Division, Library of Congress.

8. Abigail Adams to Elizabeth Shaw, 19 July 1799, Elizabeth S. Shaw Family Papers, Manuscript Division, Library of Congress.

9. *New York Times*, 11 January 1977.

ISBN 0-16-041873-9

90000

9 780160 418730